SLAVERY
IN THE
UNITED STATES

American Studies
Louis Filler, Series Editor

Slavery in the United States,
Louis Filler

SLAVERY
IN THE
UNITED STATES

Louis Filler
with a new introduction by the author

Transaction Publishers
New Brunswick (U.S.A.) and London (U.K.)

New material this edition copyright © 1998 by Transaction Publishers, New Brunswick, New Jersey 08903. Originally published in 1972 by D. Van Nostrand Company.

This book is printed on acid-free paper that meets the American National Standard for Permanence of Paper for Printed Library Materials.

Library of Congress Catalog Number: 97-48702
ISBN: 0-7658-0431-X
Printed in the United States of America

Library of Congress Cataloging-in-Publication Data

Filler, Louis, 1912–
    [Slavery in the United States of America]
    Slavery in the United States / Louis Filler ; with a new introduction by the author.
        p. cm.
    Originally published: Slavery in the United States of America. New York : Van Nostrand, 1972.
    Includes bibliographical references (p.   ) and index.
    ISBN 0-7658-0431-X (pbk. : alk. paper)
    1. Slavery—United States—History. 2. Slavery—United States—History—Sources. I. Title.
E441.F54   1998
305.5'67'0973—dc21   97-48702
                                                                       CIP

Table of Contents

Introduction to the Transaction Edition: Slavery as Labor System and as Moral Challenge

Slavery is so reprehensible to civilized minds—minds matured in complex and rationalized conditions—that they would seem unable to accept its premises without great damage to language, social organization, and individual choice. In fact, many civilized areas have by now officially denounced slavery and held it outlawed by civilized standards.

More primitive people, living by old, obsolete traditions, would appear on the surface more vulnerable to the temptations of enslavement, more likely to fall back upon it to ease their own labors, essentially to exploit those of weak mental or physical make-up as individuals or groups on various grounds of ethnic traits, strange and alien. They might so create reasons for ignoring the human wants and status of such "inferiors."

In his labor studies, the late Professor Richard B. Morris probed slavery as an institution. His studies premised slavery as an institution, a form of organization, to the annoyance of some of his graduate students, and were not offered to a larger public. Professor Morris made little effort to confront the public with the intricacies of his theory, evidently sensing that people would not be empathetic to his findings.

Yet there are emotional concepts related to slavery which touch the least academic of the general public. Rod Serling, the popular playwright, began his career with a play that depicted a white-collar worker driven to all but madness by the strategies of a superior who demeaned his contributions, allowed him inferior office space, and increasingly diminished his capacity to work. The answer to this, in Serling's play, was increased competition. It would diminish the oppressor's authority and make for a more humane business life.

Competition can of course reach formidable competitors to "enslave" them in a sense. In some cases, such as war, competitors can be forced by government to "cooperate," so that their common war can move on. Then, high position, even the highest, can be reduced, as Shakespeare has it, to little more than "ceremony." Still, though colonels and generals can die like simple soldiers there is much that separates the officer from the drafted private.

While civilization, then, carries remnants of slavery with it, more primitive civilizations may often bear their burdens more lightly. For one thing, the primitive has fewer possessions for him to quarrel over. The family ranks higher in his culture. The Bushmen of Botswana, for example, is satisfied with the communally slaughtered beast for food and water to drink. Children are precious, for love, for teaching, for the future. Circumstances are not always Edenic, but they contrast, at times fairly well, with the more pandemonic excesses of complex situations.

Today in favored Argentina, that is, in the Buenos Aires area of that large country—one-third the size of the United States—the Indians in the back stretch fight for life. Though they resist extermination they show gentler qualities to their own kind.

In earlier civilizations slavery regularly accompanied wars. The records are full of warriors and warrior kings with brothers and children fighting to supersede them. What better way to breathe the air of more expansive lands, to fight for greater satisfactions in food, clothing, and shelter? And once the war or wars ended, the victors decided, with the conquered left in the dust, that what else was there to do with the conquered but to kill the unreconciled, and divide the rest into categories—all slaves, intellectuals, artisans, household and other useful hands—and deal with the remainder as occasion suggested?

Arrangements ranged from the barbaric to the refined. Some were starved to death, for the amusement of the citizenry. Some put to labor in the fields or behind oars. One is reminded of the chances of war affecting Rome itself. Hannibal destroyed its elite forces after coming down from the Alps. Had he not hesitated, giving the desperate Romans a chance to gather new forces, he might indeed have died with his Carthaginian host. But he might instead have destroyed the regal city of Rome and changed the world's face for a considerable time. Some pangs over slaughter stirred many years later in human breasts. At least they recalled the immortal cry of gladiators in Roman arenas: *Ave Caesar.*

Morituri te salutamus! (Hail Caesar. We who are about to die salute you!) It took time to create such nuances of sensibility. As late as the end of the Punic Wars, Scipio Africanus Minor, conqueror of Carthage, could weep as he saw that noble city burning, bethinking himself that Rome could suffer a like death at some future time, as it did.

It took many centuries before slavery could reach its apogee with the discovery of the New World. The sixteenth century was filled with competitive pro-slavery nations defending their rights with powder and cannon. Spain, France, Italy, and England, and their American colonies, too, offering rum and ships, drew up treaties specifying amounts of slaves who were to be delivered via slave ships for specified amounts of gold, silver, and national currencies. It was a period of "chivalry"—partly in pride of their own heroes, caught in the networks of war, partly in regard for gallant foes, all part of new and more modern ways. None of these touched slavery, unless they were of a special caste developed over the centuries who, by reason of special conditions, special services, or features of body or mind, occupied a protected category. As late as the early eighteenth century, William Wilberforce, though opposed to slavery and sharing responsibility for its decline under English flags, was respected in the South for his intense piety. At the other extreme was John Scott, Lord Eldon, Chancellor of England, who declared in Parliament that "the slave state has been sanctioned by parliaments with the wisest legal experts, the most enlightened theologians, the most eminent statesmen."

Slaves over the centuries produced orators, advisors who taught Greek to the Latin-speaking leaders of the world. On a wider human level slavery involved women as captives who were brutalized and made prostitutes. Slaves appear in Latin plays and poems, as in the valued verses of Catullus. They are the "Figaroes" of later times: clever fellows who aided their masters and exercised a species of rule in the homes of the gentry, a group of adepts necessary to civility, if not civilization.

They were often freed by appreciative masters. They were made serfs in the Middle Ages, not very much different from slaves, but bound to the land and less likely to be torn from their kith (familiars) and kin, less likely to be uprooted or lost to family. They became "indentured" servants in England, able to work off their indentureship to freedom.

The British colonies in America gained from these changes. They absorbed an assortment of convicted criminals, often lodged in "gaols" for crimes, some of which became obsolete in time. In the colonies they could work off their indenture of seven to ten years; then, if they had

spirit, head for the frontier to contrive a new identity. Runaways sometimes left before their term had run out, thanks to the wide frontier. Andrew Johnson, who became president of the United States, was a domestic
runaway indentured servant who became a tailor in Tennessee before he
manifested qualities which hastened his rise.

During the War of Independence, British Army officials for England
purchased "Hessians" from their masters in Hesse, Germany, to act as
soldiers in the British Army. It proved a strategy that was harmful to the
British cause as appearing offensive to American patriots, though many
of them owned slaves themselves. The Hessians did their duty as soldiers, some leaving their bones in American soil. Others were "emancipated" by the peace of 1783, and melted into the general population as
free German-Americans, married to American women.

Russian serfdom was wiped out by Czarist fiat in the nineteenth century, but due to Russian backwardness continued into the twentieth century. Tolstoi saw Russians of the soil who could not understand that they
were "free"—whatever freedom could mean to benighted former serfs.

Slavery has been written up in countless books, mainly by anti-slavery
partisans. A few more or less forthright pro-slavery contenders, mainly
from seats of power, have viewed blacks as animals, heathens, creatures
to be saved for Christianity, necessary for better living, for national goals,
and other alleged reasons. It, slavery, dominates and continues to dominate ideals. It does not dominate debates. It is invidious. It appears as
rhetoric, as in "industrial slavery," but has troubles with strike breakers,
many of whom in the cities were black.

It was a difficult concept in the nineteenth century, because it was
identified with the United States, a leading country to which many slave
traders came to unload obnoxious and often sickening cargo. But it took
only a moment's honest thought to realize that slavery existed almost
everywhere to one or another degree, by family ties, the affection between slave and master or mistress, the length of service or servitude,
the depth of thralldom, bondmanship—as in Shakespeare's *The Merchant of Venice*—or drudgery, whether caste created special formalities,
how a barbarous society treated its mean chattel. Slavery was enslavement, however it was defined, taking on the rights of the seignior of the
manor or the humanity of the master.

There was a special power and question of civilization in American
slavery. It took in such disparate figures as Thomas Jefferson and Harriet
Beecher Stowe's big-fisted Tom Loker and Simon Legree, ingeniously
made a native of New England. It lay in the nation's fluid social and

economic power and capacity to change. It had settled with England in a Declaration of Independence which avoided the slavery issues; there could have been no Revolution without the South. Since then, the coalition had tested state power in congressional debates and compromise acts. It had resisted southern efforts to make the North open to slavery, removed President Buchanan from the White House—who thought he had no power to hold the South in the Union—and replaced him with Lincoln, whose first goal was to save the Union before all else. It was the soldiery that saved the Union by approving his leadership and bringing down the Confederate States of America.

Then rose voices of another kind. Wendell Phillips was a Boston aristocrat, a golden-voiced follower of William Lloyd Garrison, fire-brand of emancipation. They would have taken a chance on full emancipation while the battle raged in the fields. It was one of the unspoken secrets of the North that Lincoln's Emancipation Proclamation did not endow the blacks with full legal rights, until the 1950s produced reckless historians who would retrospectively have taken a chance on alienating the *Unionists* in slave states by attempting to impose total emancipation on them. Total emancipation came legally at last with the guns of federal troops, the legal enactments of northern legislators. And with them came the impact of the Industrial Revolution.

The South fought back from its pre-war premises. This Industrial Revolution was infamous, draining the lives of children who were labored to death under unseemly conditions in the new mills and mines—in England. Abolitionists concentrated on a war for black freedom, and once it was achieved, they retired from the scene. Not Wendell Phillips. He raised the cry against industrial slavery in America's rapidly growing cities and industrial plants. He lost the interest of those who turned their eyes away, but gained those of the rising labor interest which entered into a long and massive struggle for freedom from a new slavery.

The old slavery had involved the differences between animals and humans, their relations, too, for that matter. The new slavery brought forward questions of the duties of men to men. It spoke as the old one did not with bloody hands of income, labor conditions, the rights of women, of the old and decrepit, of children and their need of defense, of limits to war, to overbearing strength, to compassion. It was a long, drawn out war taking in multi-millions of humans on irreconcilable opposite sides, yet needing conciliation for the protection of the human races. It produced results: legal sanctions, minimum protective devices, apparent solutions. But what was secure? What was established?

The wants of industry were apparently endless; but so were the wants of labor. There were industrial "barons," and also labor "barons." Someone asked Samuel Gompers, an early labor organizer, "what was labor's goal?" "More," he responded. "And if it got more, what then?" "Still more," Gompers responded. "And then?" "More, and more again." Thus, he envisioned a society of "workers." Winston Churchill, emerging from a desperate war, and fighting an election, which he lost, observed that there were numerous labor "leaders" who were by no definition "workers." Such were the dilemmas of people who sought the meanings of the times.

LOUIS FILLER

PUBLISHER'S NOTE:

The term "Negro" is used in the text, rather than black American or African American as is now the common nomenclature. Since at the time of the original writing "Negro" was in fact in broad, common usage, it is retained for purposes of maintaining the integrity of the text.

Preface

Slavery offers a peculiar challenge to the student of American life, past and present. The temptation to respond to it in parochial fashion seems all but irresistible to some individuals: to treat it as an unmitigated nightmare from the past, or from another vantage point, as a way of life which warmly repaid slave and slaveholder in many and perhaps most cases better than did ostensibly free societies.

Another approach avoids parochial attitudes by rising "above" the challenge. The student is expected to practice objectivity removed from human considerations. He emphasizes facts and figures which may be used for any or all purposes. Still another approach is partial to intellectuality: it focuses upon hypotheses which can be projected almost in the spirit of play. Was the slave condition analogous to that of Jews in later concentration camps? Were slaveholders ridden with guilt complexes? Were abolitionists scions of formerly élite classes, and using "humanitarianism" as a tool with which to reassert an undermined social authority? One can marshal evidence for or against such suppositions, and leave them with a sense of having demonstrated his wit and expertise.

It is unreal to avoid the human implications of slavery and its practice, but it is equally unhelpful to a maturing sense of the human condition to assume glib and partial viewpoints with respect to so all-embracing a system as slavery became. It takes only a moment to realize that there were distinguished and disreputable elements on both sides of the slavery relationship, and in every part of the United States. Moreover, the cause of progress—for those who believe in progress—is not advanced by indifference to patent facts. The civil libertarian who romanticizes Negroes indiscriminately, and lumps Jefferson Davis with Simon Legree may win some popularity with enthusiasts. But he will soon find himself as quaint and as outmoded, as dependent on local affections, as some present-day sentimentalist of "Black Power" or stipendiary of the "Lost Cause."

The safest approach to slavery—as to antislavery—is national: to determine what the institution meant to the country at large: why it flourished as it did, and how it came to be opposed and overthrown. True, Daniel Webster was covered with obloquy in the North for coming before the United States Senate in 1850 to speak for Henry Clay's famous Compromise "not as a Massachusetts man, nor as a Northern man, but as an American." But a national *understanding* is not the same as a nationalistic approach. One is political, and may or may not be justified. The other attempts to grapple with the various forces which are palpably before him, and the various issues which are in controversy. These are difficult to comprehend in the best of times. If, however, one *begins* by assuming the total justice of a partial or sectional attitude, he can hardly avoid limiting his powers of growth.

LOUIS FILLER

Part I

SLAVERY IN THEORY

AND PRACTICE

CHAPTER 1

The New World and Slavery

The Problem of Slavery. Slavery came to be generally identified with Negroes. Public consciousness gradually dimmed respecting its impact upon Indians, to say nothing of white servant classes subject to the more onerous terms of indentureship. A Negro-white syndrome replaced recognition of the fact that explorers and settlers, leaders in English, French, and other provinces, and citizens of what became the United States of America, perceived life, its duties, and opportunities in particular ways.

Those ways changed under the pressure of events and the process of what has been termed "upward mobility." In time, slavery as such was outlawed by Constitutional Amendment, and became part of a closed past. And yet not wholly closed. Survivers of older times were not stilled, and produced children of power and distinction. Woodrow Wilson, John F. Harlan, William C. Dodd, William Faulkner, Douglas Southall Freeman, Hodding Carter, among countless more of national repute—artists, editors, merchants, statesmen, and others—not so much defended slavery as they did the good name of the South. They were aided by those North and South who saw the Civil War not as a moral crisis, but as an adjustment in the equation of industry and agriculture.

Yet the problem of how to estimate slavery and its workings persisted and persists. Ulrich B. Phillips in his *Life and Labor in the Old South* (1929) recaptured in admirable prose a sense of how the institution had functioned as a living, breathing entity. Kenneth Stampp's *The Peculiar Institution* (1956) retraced Phillips's course, and more critically reviewed its workings for a less empathetic era. More recently, Eugene D. Genovese, *The Political Economy of Slavery* (1965) pondered the workings of slavery as embodying dilemmas of a moral and economic nature.

3

But, aside from such analyses, how is one to treat the experiences of slavery? What approaches are appropriate to the figures, the events, the institutions of this ancient thread in human affairs? We would be poorer for a history of philosophy without Plato, a canon of poetry without Virgil, both products of slave civilizations. Shakespeare, Leonardo da Vinci, Gogol among a cloud of others were products of nations and families which lived and fulfilled themselves among slaves or serfs who were scarcely a step from slavery. If we withheld our regard from them or others who dreamed or directed governments and societies using the products of involuntary servitude, we would have to do without some, perhaps most of the greatest names of all time. At home, we would be deprived of such pillars of freedom and authority as Thomas Jefferson, George Mason (father of the Bill of Rights), and Andrew Jackson, to note three among many figures of symbolic stature. (*See Reading No. 1.*)

The easy solution is to wave them off as obsolete, and to demand freedom for all everywhere now. It is an attractive prospect, and has enchanted distinguished equalitarians throughout the ages. The problem is to define freedom, today as well as yesterday, and to determine what a living society will tolerate and accept. The best of libertarians have found it necessary or expedient to view the workings of slavery more closely. They have labored to perceive shades of differences between slaves and slaveholders, freemen and freedmen, northerners and southerners, in all the categories of work and privilege.

The Slavery Heritage. The nineteenth-century argument over the fundamental right and wrong of slavery centered over its validity as an institution in Biblical circumstances, more so than among the much admired ancient Greeks. Yet the most present-minded equalitarian could not but be aware of slavery's long, if undistinguished past. Traces of it survived in such varied concepts as *servant* and *man-servant, chattel, hand-maiden, galley slave,* and *bondage.* It suggested the fruits of victory and defeat among nations. Domestically, it referred more to a system of labor than to a moral imperative. During the critical years of the antislavery debate, northern partisans would try to expose differences between Bible slavery and that at home, to the latter's disadvantage. Southern defenders would identify themselves with Greece and Rome, describing themselves as part of a "Mediterranean civilization."

Though slavery hewed a continuous path from remotest times, rel-

atively little of its history was retained in the American consciousness. It was a curious fact of the slavery debate that then-contempo-
rary modes of enslavement in Egypt, China, Arabia, India, and
South America received meager publicity. As a popular "Treasury of
Useful Knowledge" noted, as late as 1847: "An arrangement so universal as servitude, and so conspicuous at all times, and under almost all circumstances, may be presumed to be founded in nature."

Vague echoes of enslavement in Assyrian and other early dynas-
ties were heard. Egyptian enslavement of Hebrews was recalled from
several perspectives, as was slavery among the Hebrews. That the
proud Roman Empire was based on slavery was well appreciated. So
was the treatment suffered under it by early Christians. Less fully
analyzed was the persistence of slavery under succeeding Christian
emperors. The deterioration in Europe of slave practices and traditions, and their replacement by serfdom was also obscurely ru-
mored, especially in connection with such landmarks as *Magna
Carta*. In America, the residue of historical recollection favored freedom. The tale of the gladiator Spartacus, who led a slave revolt in 73
B.C. which shook Rome, never lost its ability to excite.

The Indian as Slave and Slaver. Colonial Americans of various
nationalities fostered and indeed sponsored social discriminations
up and down the scale of humanity, of which Negroes constituted
only a minor part. One clear difference among peoples affecting the
lot of slaves separated Catholic French and Spanish from what were
mainly Protestant English pioneers and settlers. The Spanish swept
through Central America and into the Caribbean and below. They
sought the conversion of the Indians to Christianity, but they made
broad efforts to enslave them as well. So harsh and unfruitful was
the labor of Indians under their Spanish conquerors in the West Indian islands that the famous Friar Bartolomé de Las Casas, "Apostle
to the Indies," in pity urged the importation of Negro slaves from
Africa to retard the extermination of the Indians. His plea brought
thousands of Negroes to the Caribbean in 1518.

The Spanish left their marks farther north. They took "plunder
trails" into what became the American Southwest, thrusting in as far
as later Kansas. Their expeditions were accompanied by baptismal
ceremonies, but also by enslavements which became traditional not
only among Spanish and Mexicans, but among the Indians themselves.

As commerce and as social practice, slavery persisted throughout the period preceding the Civil War, and even beyond. As late as 1852, an act passed by the Territorial Legislature of Utah, "For the Relief of Indian Slaves and Prisoners," provided a milestone in a long and tragic history. It recalled the tradition of Mexican slave trading and the "common practice among these Indians to gamble away their own children and women." It noted the pitiful treatment which slaves were accorded who were taken in war or by theft, and offered legislation intended to raise their status in law and opportunity. But the document itself made it evident that family and tribal custom, as well as white-Indian differences, were likely to continue to affect Indian perspectives in the future as they had in the past.

The English were less concerned with conversion, though they were to produce notable friends of the Indians, including the saintly John Eliot of Massachusetts. In 1646 he initiated the education of Indians as part of his effort to Christianize them. For the most part his compatriots were content to best the Indians in trade, defeat them in battle, and drive them to despair. They also made efforts to enslave them, and to root Indian slavery into their economy and society, for both selfish or philanthropic purposes.

Thus Captain Israel Stoughton of Massachusetts, following an armed conflict with Indians, wrote Governor John Winthrop:

> By this pinnace, you shall receive 48 or 50 women and children, unless there stay any here to be helpful, concerning which there is one, I formerly mentioned, that is the *fairest* and *largest* among them to whom I have given a coate to cloathe her. It is my desire to have her for a servant, if it may stand to your good liking, else not. There is a little squaw that steward Culacut desireth, to whom he hath given a coate. Lieut. Davenport also desireth one, to wit, a small one, that has three strokes upon her stomach. . . . He desireth her, if it will stand upon your good liking. Sosomon, the Indian, desireth a young little squaw, which I know not.

In 1637, Roger Williams petitioned Winthrop in different vein:

> It having againe pleased the Most High to put into your hands another miserable drove of Adams degenerate seede, & our brethren by nature, I am bold (if I may not offend in it) to request the keeping & bringing up of one of the children. I have fixed mine eye on this little one with the red about his neck, but I will not be peremptory in my choice, but will rest in your loving pleasure for him or any,&c.

Laws covering the workings of Indian enslavement were extremely detailed. They varied from colony to colony. They specified groups and individuals whose freedom was limited or protected, by virtue of a colony's attitude toward either Indians or slavery. Thus the Province of New York separated free Indian inhabitants from those brought from the Spanish West Indies. Laws changed, as when in 1688, the English council in New York resolved "that all Indian slaves within this province subject to the King of Spain, that can give an account of their Christian faith and say the Lord's Prayer, be forthwith set at liberty, and sent home by the first conveyance, and likewise them that shall hereafter come to the province."

Generally, the Indian did not flourish as a slave to the English or other foreigners. His temperament, his habits of life, and what might today be called "expectations" do not appear to have fitted him for a servile place in the larger American economy. Indians as slaves to other Indians there were indeed, and also Negroes as slaves to Indians. However that might be, they responded differently to the English. Their status as original tenants of the land doubtless contributed to their frustration in the slave role. They died in battle or in bondage, submitted to the reservation life—the earliest American reservation being set up in 1786—or moved or were driven west. They assumed a subordinate role in American life, perhaps more so than did the Negroes, which has continued to the present.

Was slavery among Indians a defensible institution? Some abolitionists would later argue that the slavery they so vehemently opposed in the 1830–1860 period differed in kind from some forms of earlier enslavement, and also from slavery among contemporary Cherokees and Choctaws. They would insist that these systems of slavery constituted variations on tribal and family relations. They would contrast it to the slavery practiced by white southerners upon Negroes as "unmitigated," that is, as offering no avenues of human progress and hope to the blacks. Other abolitionists denied this view as a fantasy, especially as it pertained to the Indians. (*See Reading No. 2.*)

Indentureship and slavery. Most formidable during its long tenure—vastly more formidable, it appeared, than Negro enslavement —was the practice of *indentured servitude:* not ordinarily recognized as a slavery system, but involving elements which placed it in comparable categories. The famous New England Confederation (1643–1684), precursor of the later Revolutionary alliance, was created in part for assault and defense against Indians, in part to facilitate the return of fugitive slaves.

There were numerous forms of labor practiced by indentured servants (generally known as *kids*). Those forms varied from rigid conditions of servitude to relatively "free" labor. They took in "redemptioners," who sold their services for a period of years in order to have their passage paid to America. They included also apprentices, such involuntary laborers as convicts and debtors, and others. All worked "from sun-up to sun-down," their ease or opportunities to develop being subject to the peccadilloes of their masters. George Washington, in his youth, was taught by a convict servant whom his father bought for a schoolmaster. The constant need for labor in America tempted employers to wink at the pretentions of runaways from other colonies who claimed to be free. Indentured servitude as such gave way to the system of artisans and apprentices. But before it did, it had established norms of labor relations which ruled colonial times.

It was probably the success which attended indentured servitude, as well as the better perceived factors of rocky soil and Puritan tenets which discouraged Negro slavery in the North and made it easier to dislodge by practice and legislation. Even so, it is desirable to recall that Negro slavery in the original northern colonies persisted far beyond the American Revolution, thanks to the system of gradual emancipation which, for example, officially ended slavery in New York State in 1827, though proclaimed in 1799.*

Even so, remnants of the system of slavery proper undoubtedly persisted in the North. Thus, Sojourner Truth's owner in upper New York illegally sold her child of five years of age, he being transported south to Alabama. She herself was assured of freedom a year before Emancipation, but her master repudiating his promise on specious grounds, she was ordered to serve a year beyond the legal date. Only

---

* New York City had the distinction of having nurtured the most serious of alleged slave insurrectionary plots, that of 1741, rumors of which cost the lives of 31 Negroes, including the burning alive of 13, and the transportation of more than twice as many to the West Indies. It is significant of the identification of northern states with freedom that this "insurrection" should have been substantially forgotten, along with its alleged leaders, insurrection being more readily related to southern circumstances and locales.

escape and the generous help of strangers prevented her further exploitation.

What is important to note is that indentured servitude and associated legal agreements between master and worker were in fact *servitude*, and so universally understood. Runaway servants were sought in precise fashion as were runaway slaves.

One landmark in the decay of these institutions—at least, from hindsight—was the fleeing of Andrew Johnson in 1824 from the terms of his bound apprenticeship. A runaway from his master, a tailor in his native Raleigh, North Carolina, Johnson was advertised and sought, a reward of ten dollars being put upon him. This unlettered fugitive began life anew as a tailor in Greeneville, Tennessee. He became a sheriff, a mayor, a governor, a United States Senator, and a leader of the Homestead movement of 1846 and after, before attaining higher distinctions. But even before the saga of Andrew Johnson began, indentured servitude proper produced its prodigies: two signers of the Declaration of Independence, George Taylor of Pennsylvania and Matthew Thornton of New Hampshire, had been white servants.

White Slaves. Those who ponder the bitter lot of Negro slaves can sharpen perspective by reviewing that of the white slaves. They were preferred to free labor because of the high price the latter fetched in America. They accepted the harsh sweeping terms of indentureship because their prospects in the New World had been painted in inaccurately glowing terms, because they lacked money to come independently by ship, because they had been felons and ordered transported, or because they had been kidnapped and spirited on board ship for service in America.

Once here, their careers were at the mercy of circumstances. A kind master or a cruel one, an intelligent master or a stupid one, could make all the difference. But whether one or the other, their labors were long and arduous, and not to be distinguished in any particular from that of Negro slaves. Like them, on the lower levels of employment, they cleared the land and worked the crop. Because the terms of indentureship were limited to four to seven years, they could expect to be worked harder than servants who were owned for life.

They were talented servants and inept ones, but the majority of them, if not already so, were toughened and brutalized by their lot. A famous bit of verse by Ebenezer Cook, a tobacco agent, *The Sot*

Weed Factor or a Voyage to Maryland (1708) sees them at their rude sports and reflects their thoughts and fancies. Thus, Cook sees some coarse woman servants, dirty and harsh, quarrelling and at play. One calls to another:

> D—n you, . . . tho' now so brave
> I knew you late a Four-Years Slave;
> What if for Planter's Wife you go,
> Nature designed you for the Hoe.

And another, pretending perhaps to be a chambermaid—a rung up the social and economic ladder from field hand—muses:

> In better Times, e'er to this Land
> I was unhappily trapann'd;
> Perchance as well I did appear,
> As any Lord or Lady here. . . .
> But things are changed, now at the Hoe
> I daily work, and Barefoot go,
> In weeding Corn or feeding Swine,
> I spend my melancholy Time.
> Kidnap'd and Fool'd, I thither fled,
> To Shun a hated Nuptial Bed,
> And to my cost already find,
> Worse Plagues than those I left behind.

"Christian servants" were as a matter of course and legal restriction given releases from indentureship, and so contributed to the growing numbers of free laborers and new proprietors. The process broke down in the case of Negroes, who had themselves heretofore been part of the system, and in many recorded cases become freemen and landowners. One Anthony Johnson, a Negro, brought early to Virginia, was emancipated, and prospered sufficiently to become the master of two white servants. This essentially equalitarian system did not create a tradition linking Negro destinies with those of their white counterparts. Instead, a series of lawsuits and enactments between 1640 and 1660 established the inferior status of Negroes and removed their prerogatives as Christians as well as citizens. Such discrimination did not result from an imposing number of Negroes. There were no more than some 300 of them in Virginia in 1648. By 1700 there have been estimated to have been no more than some 20,000 Negro slaves in all the mainland English colonies. Other, additional factors determined the moral and economic developments of slavery, North and South.

CHAPTER 2

Negroes and Slavery

First Negroes not Slaves. Slavery was practiced among Negroes in Africa, as well as among Europeans, during the thousand years which followed the fall of Rome. It was also practiced among the Mohammedan peoples of north Africa; their civilizations teemed with white as well as black slaves. The factors causing the swift decline of slavery in Europe insured its not being reintroduced, after the African west coast had been opened to slavery. The major impediment to a renewed slave trade in Europe was a vast and sturdy peasant class able to bear the heavy burden of European labor, and unwilling to have its hopes of status and dignity compromised by the presence of a wholly servile class engaged in the same work as its own.

The Portuguese were the first to bring Negro slaves to the New World, carrying them into the Caribbean Sea early in the sixteenth century. More than a century passed before the mainland was visited by slavers. A Dutch ship of war brought a cargo of Negroes to Jamestown, Virginia in 1619, and exchanged them for provisions. In that year, too, the first representative body in America, the House of Burgesses, was created in the colony.

Thus, two powerful traditions were set in motion. One pointed to discriminations among people. The other, for all its partiality to owners of property, provided for possibilities of self-expression and advancement among people.

As has been seen, servitude itself was no novelty, and, indeed, no laws lent early support to slave relations, or were designed to hold blacks or whites in a state of slavery. The first Negroes in Virginia were, apparently, assimilated into the general population of freed servants. The practice and tradition of, in effect, buying off one's servitude by labor continued indefinitely. Moreover, laws protected blacks as well as whites in their character of Christians. While ordinances accumulated in the 1660's to limit the rights of Negroes and institutionalize their status, their purpose appears to have been more social than economic. As late as the 1690's, colonial legislatures felt it necessary, apparently because of variations in public understanding, to emphasize that baptism did not free a slave. Such developments were in any case still matters of secondary importance in colonial affairs. In Virginia, for example, in 1700, there were no more than about 6,000 slaves. The great center of the growing slave trade was elsewhere: in the English West Indies, where sugar growing was so lucrative as to make the very word "sugar" equivalent to money. Slaves were transported to mainland points as a byproduct of this most profitable traffic.

Yet 1700 did mark a turning point in its American history, since slave trading had been controlled by a monopoly, the Royal African Company. The ending of this monopoly in 1698 quickened a free enterprise impulse in slave trading: one which brought new thousands of Negroes to colonies from the Carolinas to Massachusetts—Negroes who found their lot increasingly separated from that of white slaves.

The Middle Passage. Cases can be cited to buttress opposing moral and historical viewpoints respecting many aspects of slavery. Numerous Evangelicals, for example—professing Christians who felt it their religious duty to promulgate Biblical truth as they understood it—accepted the argument that enslavement could be seen as a middle ground for the Christianization of Africa. Others denounced this argument. William Wilberforce, one of the most distinguished of Evangelicals, whom no slaveholder thought to deride, became an antislavery symbol. Abolitionists repudiated the Christianizing argument as offensive and false. But it was impressive to persons who supported the missionary role of civilized nations above all other goals. (*See Reading No. 3.*)

No one, however, has made efforts to defend the treatment Negroes were accorded on *slave ships,* from points of departure on the Slave Coast of Africa to arrival in western ports. The "Middle Passage"—the crossing of the Atlantic Ocean—meant that slave holds would be cruelly congested to carry a maximum number of unfortunate men, women, and children. Neither "loose" packing of slaves nor the incredible "tight" packing during the long sea voyage offered much to the humanity of the seamen or their oppressed cargo. Only a dulled moral sense could enable the former to enforce their brutal discipline and deal with their victims as beasts. Only a willingness to evade the facts kept those who protested the traffic in the press and to Parliament impotent and unable to stir public outrage. The story of the "Middle Passage" ranks with the worst infamies of history.

No aspect of it survives examination: the chains and immobility which deprived the victims of human circumstances and needs; the filth; the sickness and epidemics which were met only with fear of infection; the tragic "dancing" and forced singing of the slaves on deck, under guns and whips, in order to revive blood circulation; and the swift readiness to "jettison" slaves, that is, cast them overboard for reasons ranging from sickness to rebellion. Crucial to this aspect of slave administration were insurance contracts by which damages could not be collected if "cargo" died aboard ship. Not until 1781 did a British court explicitly decide, in a case of wholesale jettisoning of slaves, that though they were indeed merchandise, they were unlike horses, and that damages for drowned slaves would not be granted.

It needs to be recalled that though slaves were thus denied their humanity, they did represent valuable property, and that slavers made efforts to preserve it intact, during lengthy and difficult voyages in ships of limited space and facilities. Indeed, the incidence of death by sickness, close contact, frailty, response to ocean conditions, and other factors on ships carrying indentured servants (and even free Irish, Scots, and Germans) in shipholds was also high and elicited little pity or concern. They also suffered filth and discomfort, indifference and cruelty. And, in the course of months of travel, through heavy seas and storms, consigned their dead regularly to the sea.

Through the early part of the nineteenth century, various nations agreed officially to outlaw the ocean trade in slaves. The United States and England led the way, with other European nations falling in line. In 1850, Brazil, the greatest receiver of slaves, joined this concert of nations. Yet *slavers* continued to roam the seas, evading British searching parties and attracting undercover cooperation and profits from slave-dealers and even government agents. United States slavers continued to flourish. In the 1850's, as part of this program for vindicating slavery, southern spokesmen demanded the official reopening of the slave traffic, under "free trade" slogans. Thereafter, the worldwide trade in slaves continued but under hidden and obscure auspices.*

The Factor of Color. The decisive, determining quality was color, but not color alone. Many peoples around the world were "colored—a majority of them. Most of them practiced forms of slavery, upon themselves and others. Some, like the Spanish, though swarthy, were of such regal heritage and national power as not to suffer enslavement, except through misadventure or at the hands of Barbary pirates. The Indians, though "colored," were in the main crushed and driven out of their possessions. Yet their conquerors— in part, perhaps, because they had successfully resisted enslavement —mixed honor with contempt, and created the myth of the "noble savage." No such accolade was accorded Negroes, though colonial and subsequent eras produced among slaves as well as the free, Negroes of distinction: soldiers, educators, ministers, inventors, and others.

The coming slavery debate would bring forth arguments "proving" that Negroes were by nature fitted for slavery. These arguments failed to explain why slavery had not been unique to Africans. They passed over the fact that Negroes, made chattels, often found escape through suicide, madness, fatal depression, and other means available on or off slave ships. They ignored the fact that the withering of slavery in northern states found free and emancipated Negroes as concerned for advancing their privileges as any other social group. Most significantly, they failed to cope with the long, continuous record of race mixture—*miscegenation,* as it would later be termed— which created vast confusion and contradictions, most of which ardent racists found it expedient to evade in debate.

Enslavement North and South. Slavery advanced slowly, but linked itself firmly with social, economic, and religious presumptions. Thus William Byrd II of Westover Plantation, Virginia, probably ranked the Irish no higher than the Negroes, and may have felt more affection for the latter. He judged it the "lowest Prostitution" for a gentlewoman to have stooped to marrying a "Hibernian" who had been her uncle's overseer. Byrd's views were based on class attitudes: his sense of the duties owed by individuals to family and soci-

* For an important study in the field, Philip D. Curtin, *The Atlantic Slave Trade: A Census* (Madison, Wis., 1969).

tudes: his sense of the duties owed by individuals to family and society. Others of less élite status than Byrd were as quick as he to judge their masters and inferiors. The fate of Negroes in the new world was determined by such pressures and events, in and out of their own communities.

Their status varied from province to province, and later from state to state. Slaves were freely offered for purchase North and South, and took on functions defined by local conditions. (*See Reading No. 4.*) They became chiefly house servants in Massachusetts, and at least in law and religion, if not in practice, were seen as requiring human regard. Crispus Attucks, later made famous in the Boston Massacre, was a runaway slave in 1750, who appears to have voluntarily returned to his master in Framingham, Massachusetts where he worked with a certain freedom and confidence. The rocky soil of New England found little use for slave laborers, and the heightened effectiveness of labor-saving devices contributed to a generally increasing disrespect for slave labor.

The feudal domains of the Hudson Valley in New York were more receptive to slaves in number and in farm employment. Yet the independent farmers who dreamed of owning without restriction patroon's land which they tilled dreamed less of owning slaves in aggregate. Pennsylvania became the classic case of a state so well served by indentured servants, especially German who worked their way to freedom, as to find slavery distasteful. Though Pennsylvania attracted a relatively large number of slaves, it was more prompt than New York to provide for *gradual emancipation*, and to liquidate the system, though not always with the former slaves' best interests in view.

Overall, the North was more significant for its role in the transportation of slaves, than for its furtherance of slavery institutions. Northern ships, based in Massachusetts, Rhode Island, and New York ports supported the famous or notorious "triangular trade," bringing rum to slave factories on the west African coast, and receiving for it a human cargo which was brought ashore in the West Indies. There it was exchanged for molasses, later so fateful in British-colonial relations. Slaves were then transported to mainland points, for auction or consignment, and the molasses brought home for the further manufacture of rum.

North and South were so intricately related, commercially and socially, so far as Negroes were concerned, that it would be (and continues to be) a major problem to determine precisely what it was that drew North and South apart—what made possible so colossal a brother's war as finally materialized.

CHAPTER 3

The "Peculiar Institution"

Slavery in the South. North and South blended into what would become the Border States, where questions of slavery and attitudes toward Negroes became not more complex, but more demanding. Delaware and Maryland were southern in sentiment, but their contiguity with Pennsylvania and New Jersey created disturbing internal differences on questions of national policies and treatment of Negroes. Slaveholders and libertarians lived side by side in these states, making general agreement on definitions of servitude and freedom difficult. Roger B. Taney, of Maryland was one of the most ardent of Jacksonians, an enemy of monopoly, a key figure in the celebrated battle against the Second Bank of the United States. In his youth, he also spoke with contempt of the slavery system and expressed hopes for its early demise. Later, as Chief Justice of the United States Supreme Court, in his *Dred Scott Decision* (1857), he attempted to nationalize the institution, and thus helped precipitate the Civil War.

Virginia, bastion of the expanding South, revealed in its geography its basic social and economic inclinations. Its lowlands were lush, suitable for plantations, slave labor, and the growth of a distinguished Tidewater aristocracy. In its western highlands, however, leading over to the Ohio River, would gather pioneers and independent farmers less regardful of slaves as property than were their more gracious eastern compatriots, and more willing to rid themselves of slavery establishments, if this could be accomplished with no violence to their interests. Much the same could be said of those who early passed over into Kentucky by way of the Appalachians and the Ohio Valley, and later in full emigration through the Cumberland Gap.

Slavery in North Carolina showed a similar process creating large plantations east, and, in the western mountains, smaller freeholds.

(*See Reading No. 5.*) South Carolina, however, with its superb harbors, attained rapid affluence based on massive slave holdings. It developed a stately view of the distance separating not only slaves from freemen, but gentlemen from the more humble Blue Ridge and Upland farmers. However, South Carolina's relatively small size and influx of English Dissenters and French Huguenots helped create in its leaders a keen sense of independence and sensitivity to criticism which would make them fierce defenders of what they deemed their way of life.

Georgia, founded late in 1732 by General James Oglethorpe, was initiated as a philanthropic experiment in part (it was intended also to create a buffer state opposing Spanish Florida), and it forbade slavery. However, the settlers, themselves often of mean circumstances, increasingly demanded a labor supply of Negroes, and in 1750 the ban upon slaves was lifted.

Growth of a "Money Crop." The infant Virginia colony was once saved by tobacco: a tenacious, durable, easily grown weed which had given the hard pressed settlers a *staple crop,* readily barrelled and exchanged in England for the manufactured goods they desired. It also committed them to an unfavorable balance of trade with London and Glasgow merchants with whom they became legally and traditionally bound to trade. Tobacco drained their soil of vital nutriments, thus ensuring that they would have to expand their land holdings into new territories.

Such factors encouraged dependence on a slave economy: one of large gangs of workers in the fields, the warehouses, and on the levees. Other staples similarly absorbed great numbers of rudely differentiated slaves: hands for seeding, tending, hoeing, picking, and carrying. Rice, indigo, sugar, corn (a food staple) and a few other products preempted land in the South which could have sustained the soil and challenged the necessity for slaves. Southern planters did not study closely, as a class, crop rotation and other aspects of scientific farming.

The staple of staples, however, ultimately became cotton, though its future was uncertain in the years before the invention of the cotton gin. Tearing the cotton from the seed was a difficult process, especially when using "short-staple" cotton. ("Sea-island" cotton was easily separated, but needed water and could only be grown off the coasts of South Carolina and Georgia, creating special conditions for the slaves affected.) The invention of the cotton gin by Eli Whitney in 1793 overcame the problem retarding the use of short-staple cotton, and made it available for wide cultivation. The economics of cotton production, as of slavery in general, have been questioned in all eras. Nevertheless, plantation owners turned to it with enthusiasm. Rice was grown in South Carolina. Tobacco continued to be cultivated in Virginia, North Carolina, Maryland, and Kentucky. Sugar became a major product of Louisiana planters. But slaveholders increasingly poured human and material resources into developing the new staple, and from Virginia to Texas made their section the Land of Cotton.

While slavery withered in the North, it expanded below the Mason and Dixon Line. By the time of the American Revolution, there were some half a million slaves distributed throughout the colonies. Of these, there were perhaps no more than fifty thousand in the North. Farther south, the great bulk of them were in Virginia and the Carolinas.

CHAPTER 4

Effects of Revolutionary and Post-Revolutionary Eras

The Future of Slavery in Suspension. Possibly Great Britain could have ended slavery in the colonies by the simple expedient of consistently releasing slaves, wherever its troops were lodged in rebel territory, from Massachusetts to Georgia. Such a policy, in addition, would have comported with British policy at home. In 1772, in the Somerset case, Lord Mansfield had ruled that England's free soil could not tolerate the presence of slavery, and ordered the release of a slave brought from Virginia to the home country. Although this decision did not affect the destinies of slaves elsewhere, notably in the West Indies, it furnished a precedent which could have changed the course of history. (*See Reading No. 6, for a comparison with the problem of the Emancipation Proclamation.*) Unfortunately, the British commanders in America were blinded by self-interest, and, rather than turning slaves against their masters, preferred to seize many of them for transportation and sale in Jamaica and elsewhere.

Although humanitarian sentiments opposing slavery had heretofore been elicited mainly from distinguished northerners and Quakers, slaveholders South as well as North had long protested the foreign slave trade which bound them to slavers from Bristol, England, to Bristol, Rhode Island. Virginia prided herself on her many resolutions pleading for an end to the traffic. These were disallowed by the King's Privy Council on grounds that suppression of the slave trade would close off a valuable and benign industry.

Whether Virginians, and especially South Carolinians, were more concerned for its immorality or harbored a growing fear of slave insurrections, can never be wholly determined. In addition, it may be noted that although southerners accepted British rulings on the slave trade, at least until the Revolutionary era, they were less flexible in their resistance to the Navigation Acts, which frustrated many of their economic ambitions. Moreover, Virginia itself was becoming more and more a breeding place for slaves to be sold farther south and west. The state thus had a competitor's repugnance to the distresses of the Middle Passage. The Declaration of Independence denounced the Crown for supporting this "execrable Commerce," but it also denounced it for having "excited domestic insurrections amongst us."

Nevertheless, the era of the Revolution was also a period of hope that slavery might fall of its own inadequacies. Not a few slaveholders *manumitted* their slaves, that is, gave them their freedom, in order to carry on their own revolt with free hands. Numerous slaves were manumitted for outstanding services against the British. On the other hand, one of the sad incentives offered volunteers in the Continental Army—a major incentive was free land—was slave property of their own.

The record of Negroes during the Revolution was mixed. Perhaps as many sought to better themselves by siding with the British forces as remained loyal to their revolutionary masters. The victory of the latter was a defeat for their hopes, though probably not for their real opportunities. In the main, their service with Tories gives one measure of the looseness of the patriarchal bonds which southerners had been forging for almost a century.

Advance of Freedom and Slavery. The repulse of British arms, the deeds of the foot soldier, including the Negro soldier with whom the white one ate and lived freely while at war, the promise of the new industry repugnant to slave labor—all this fed expectations that slavery would crumble in the South as it had in the North. Many southern leaders, eager to rid themselves of their dependence on English and northern merchants and manufacturers, approved the trend toward free labor and sought to further it.

Thomas Jefferson was among the foremost in conceiving plans to prevent slavery expansion. During the Confederation period, he fathered the Northwest Ordinance of 1787, intended to provide a governmental framework for American lands east of the Mississippi River and north of the Ohio. One of its momentous provisions excluded slavery from its borders. Less well-known is the projected *Southwest* Ordinance, affecting territories which became Alabama and Mississippi, Tennessee and Kentucky. This earlier motion, en-dorsed by George Washington, Patrick Henry, James Madison, and George Mason would have sealed off slavery from western expansion and encouraged dreams of closing out its holdings in the eastern states. Tragically, although the vote stood fifteen to six in the Confederated Congress favoring the proposal, it failed to gain the requisite nine states, and was lost.*

The Federal Constituion of 1787 was enigmatic about the future of slavery, as of other matters. It was an arena for the struggle of opposing social and economic interests which it was intended to mediate, rather than a mandate for specific action. Nevertheless, although the Constitution did not mention slaves by name, it included them as "three fifths of all other persons" (Art. I, sec. 2), in granting slaveholders congressional representation based on their slave constituency, as well as on free people. Slavery also shadowed the Constitution in its provision (Art. IV, sec. 2) allowing the extradition of fugitive slaves.

Invention of the Cotton Gin. The decisive blow fell in 1793 when, as earlier noted, Eli Whitney invented the cotton gin, answering the question of whether cotton growing could be made a source of wealth. It was significant of southern responsiveness to industry that this major mechanical breakthrough should not have inspired, as mechanical breakthroughs did in the North, a new enthusiasm for free labor. Ironically, it has been suggested that it was slave ingenuity on the plantation which first conceived the technical details for separating the lint from the seed, elements which Whitney refined in assembling his invention. Thereafter, the manumission of slaves fell precipitously.

Yet the blow to abolitionist hopes fell softly. The 1790's continued to be an era of hope. The Constitutional provision (Art. I, sec. 9) permitting the ending of the foreign slave trade in 1808 was duly enacted into law. The speed-up of gradual emancipation in the North, the expectation that Kentucky would voluntarily end slavery within its borders—Henry Clay participated in this vain effort—and the Jeffersonian rhetoric of freedom throughout this time, all contributed to a tolerance and acceptance of the actual institutionalization of slavery in the South.

---

* Even less known is the fact that slavery in the Northwest continued a full quarter century after passage of the Northwest Ordinance, and perished of attrition rather than law.

CHAPTER 5

Stabilizing the Slave System

Slave and Black Codes. A body of laws governing slaves accumulated which had as its goals policing and suppressing blacks. Some of the provisions of the law were barbaric, and startled northern readers, when they were later called to their attention. For the most part, such laws were anachronistic, rather than deliberately malevolent. Branding and burning at the stake, for example, had been acceptable measures of social control in colonial days, when different standards of social life were universally accepted. Some slave-control laws were cruel and inhuman, rather than barbaric, and, to be properly assayed, need to be compared with general measures elsewhere governing murder, theft, sexual assaults, breaking contracts, and other social relations.

The theory and practice of the Slave Code were debated. Abolitionists held that the established law unleashed the worst impulses of the master. Theodore D. Weld's later influential *American Slavery as It Is: The Testimony of a Thousand Witnesses* (1839) extracted items from southern newspapers to reveal its day to day pitilessness. Southern defenders retorted that a similar volume of a more horrendous stripe could be readily compiled from northern papers, revealing heartlessness and inequity displayed toward the black and white poor. Moreover, they asserted, the actual practice of slavery was benign and involved a personal regard for Negroes that was unknown in the North.

However the Slave Code was interpreted, there could be no doubting its purpose: to preserve the individual slaveholder's right in his slave as property and to ensure the slave's helplessness in conceiving or furthering insurrectionary actions. In implementation of the Slave Code, white southerners developed the voluntary institution of patrols—known to slaves as "paterollers"—which were composed of private citizens, ready at a moment's notice to arm and meet at designated points for vigilante purposes. Such patrols were composed of all ranks of white citizens. Decades of experience with patrols were credited in part with having produced the strikingly high percentage of competent officers and soldiers which the Confederacy of 1861–1865 was able to put into the field.

The Slave Code was developed to include highly refined details of conduct, based on definitions of negritude, acceptable attitudes between white and black individuals and rights, and privileges in court cases. These were particularly necessary because of the presence of free Negroes in southern states. Approximately one Negro in every eight was free, and the number of free blacks were equally divided between North and South. In both instances, their governance was more properly perceived under Black Codes, rather than Slave Codes. (*See Reading No. 7.*) However, in the South, the dominant condition of Negroes being slavery, it controlled the actions and prospects of free Negroes as well as their technically more humble brethren.

Like the slave, the free Negro's lot depended on social tolerance. Like the slave, too, the free Negro required a patron to help him resist malice or antagonism. He was often subject to a more calculated contempt, intended to remind him of his limited status. And over him hung at all times, in the South, the threat of re-enslavement, as a result of alleged crime, accusations of having aided runaways, and other charges. There were even recorded cases of free Negroes who voluntarily sought enslavement, in order, as they thought, to improve their circumstances.

Black Codes in the North also afflicted Negroes, and were perhaps as disheartening because of the sharp contrast between ideals of freedom more readily encountered, as byproducts of political rhetoric, and the realities of discrimination and antagonism, unqualified by paternalism. (*See Reading No. 8.*)

Slavery at Home and Abroad. The course of slavery elsewhere did not so much affect American slavery as it did provide a contrast to it. Most significant was the British example which, for a while, seemed to parallel American developments. In both countries, repugnance to the African slave trade roused philanthropic sentiments, and in 1807, by a coincidence, both Congress and Parliament officially outlawed it, to take effect the following year.

The forces in Great Britain defending and resisting the slave trade were both conservative in interests and social outlook. Lord Dartmouth, President of the Board of Trade and opposed to abolition, was pious enough to be nicknamed "The Psalm-Singer." His adversary, William Wilberforce, as noted before, bore one of the most admired names in the western world.*

The key difference between British and American circumstances was that British slaves toiled abroad, in the Caribbean and in India, while those of Americans were influenced by local control and by states rights. (*See Reading No. 9.*) This vital difference made it certain that conservatives and radicals in both countries, though they influenced each other, would no more be able to join hands with their own kind across the sea than they had been able to in order to avert a revolutionary war. In addition, both peoples were affected in their attitudes toward slavery by the careers of slavery elsewhere.

* It needs to be recalled from time to time what a torch of freedom and opportunity the United States seemed to present to the world, as compared to suppression abroad. William Cobbett, the Tory Radical, had a career in both England and the United States, and developed a love of American institutions. He despised Wilberforce as a "canting saint," who felt for Negroes afar but had no feeling for the "factory slaves" at home. In Cobbett's vivid prose, on having returned to the United States:

> "To see a free country for once, and to see every labourer with plenty to eat and drink! Think of *that!* And never to see the hang-dog face of a tax-gatherer. Think of *that!* No Alien Acts here! No long-sworded and whiskered Captains. No judges escorted from town to town and sitting under the guard of dragoons. No packed juries of tenants. . . . No hangings and rippings up. . . . No Cannings, Liverpools, Castlereaghs. . . . No Wilberforces. Think of *that!* No Wilberforces!" (*Cobbett's Weekly Political Register,* XXXIV [1818], 215.)

CHAPTER 6

Spanish and American Slavery Compared

"Open" Societies and "Closed" Societies. It has been argued that Spanish rule, as in Cuba, and Portuguese rule in Brazil produced more defensible brands of slavery, because of their regard for the Catholic needs of their servants, and their greater willingness to mix and intermarry with them. The American South, on the other hand, became a "closed society," not unlike a much later concentration camp, requiring its slaves to live the double lives of non-people and suppressed revolutionaries.

The argument tends to fall into rigid theory and emotional thinking. It tends to forget or romanticize the hopelessly impoverished, religion and caste-ridden, dictatorial nature of the supposedly more "free" Latin-American nations. It sees the American South, and its Negro populations, too, in more simplistic terms than their actual history warrants. In truth, South American nations, in overthrowing Spanish and Portuguese rule, found it relatively easy to abolish formal slavery. In practice, however, their rituals of freedom left almost everything yet to be done to advance socially individual dignity and opportunity.

Fluid Aspects of Southern Society. Brilliant Negro and half-caste liberators and poets were indeed produced in South American nations. Their vast slave revolts and exalted apostrophes to freedom were, however, less indications of a growing tradition of liberty and equality than of under-development, tyrants, and anarchy. In contrast, the American South did, certainly, develop a tradition of repression which finally reached crisis proportions. But it also developed a tradition of liberty. The National Period (from the Revolution to the Era of Good Feelings [1820–1824]) was one of hope and expansion, from which not all, but some Negroes gained, and all Negroes fed. European visitors who did not come in order to patronize the American barbarians often noted that slaves ate better than freemen of Europe and Great Britain.

The national era seemed far from rigid for Negroes. It produced efforts to prepare Negroes for colonization experiments, in which Jefferson, Lafayette, and others cooperated. It produced notable denunciations of slavery by such influential leaders as John Wesley, and a succession of famous Negroes, some identified with slavery. Manumission societies, with attendant educational and other philanthropic functions, were vigorous in the upper South, from which, it was expected, abolitionist programs would radiate still further south. "As late as 1840 there were more intelligent blacks in the South than in the North." *

Frances Wright's Nashoba, Tennessee, experiment in communal living was attended by Negroes as well as whites. *Miscegenation,* the relationship of men and women of one race with partners of the opposite sex of a different race, continued throughout the era, despite harsh social sanctions. Richard M. Johnson of Kentucky, a hero of the War of 1812 and Martin Van Buren's Vice-President, had a daughter by Julia Chinn, a mulatto whom he acquired when his father's estate was settled. Wilberforce University in southwestern Ohio was later, in 1856, created in part to serve the mulatto children of southern slaveholders. An untold number of Negroes "passed" into white society as occasion required or permitted, in fashions which elements of other ethnic groups repeated.

Not to be derogated, also, as a process which created new freedmen from former slaves was the buying of freedom by slaves, through extra labors or a particular understanding between master and slave: a practice which harked back to indentureship. An additional practice among free Negroes was to raise money by special labors, philanthropic support, or door-to-door appeals which would enable them to purchase relatives out of slavery.

That repression of slave talents accompanied American affluence and expansion cannot and ought not to be denied. But it would be as inaccurate to portray their lot as, for example, uniformly equivalent to that of the victims of concentration camp or forced labor sit-

---

* C. G. Woodson, *The Education of the Negro Prior to 1861* (Washington, D.C., 1919 ed.), 235. This work by the "father of Negro History" merits a note of its own, being a masterpiece of research and effort to display the facts without evasion or unseemly special pleading.

uations. Concentration camps were vehicles for punishment, and sought to hide their inner workings rather than to display them. The circumstances of the expansion era offered opportunities to all, in one or another degree. When they ceased to do so—as happened in the 1830's—the most urgent among white antislavery southerners were forced to depart for northern homes. Desperate Negroes of talent and sensibility took the road of the fugitive slave, and enriched the North with their presence.

How much real potential for freedom there was in the southern states, as between Negroes and whites, can probably never be known. Henry Clay, as Secretary of State in the administration of John Quincy Adams, dreamed of a Pan-American Union, for which he continues to be honored south of the American border. The dream was suppressed by southern followers of Andrew Jackson, in part because they were unwilling to give diplomatic courtesies to governments which included Negroes and mulattoes. Such critical decisions suggest the limits to freedom and association which southerners shared.

Compensated Emancipation. The British example of abolition in the West Indies strangely failed to inspire substantial demand that the same be done at home. Years of agitation in Parliament finally enabled it to set aside £20 million to purchase peacefully the freedom of the nation's West Indian slaves. How much actual "freedom" the great redemption won would be debated by southern skeptics and northern enthusiasts until the Civil War came. However, a similar movement in the United States would have averted the Civil War. It would have united the nation by recognizing that both North and South had been implicated in the long history of domestic slavery. It would have spread the cost of freeing the slaves over the entire nation, and done away with questions about the justice of burdening slaveholders with the entire financial cost of the operation.

All this could have been done painlessly at the mere expense of selling part of the western lands the nation owned in such abundance, in order to meet the expenses of slave purchase and of giving the freed Negroes a new and proper beginning in American society.

None of this was to be. Western immigrants from the North and the South demanded free homesteads. As late as the coming of the Civil War itself, the despairing efforts of the great pacifist Elihu Burritt to prevent hostilities by means of a compensation plan were frustrated by simple lack of interest and support in the North. Southerners were even more contemptuous of the scheme. They scorned the results of British emancipation, "proving" that it, and subsequent apprenticeship systems, worked badly and resulted in deteriorated social and labor conditions.

They scorned, too, Negro uprisings in Haiti as evidence of what savagery emancipation must unleash. While William Wordsworth in his radical youth, and Wendell Phillips in his abolitionist maturity wrote of the revolutionary leader Toussaint L'Ouverture with surpassing eloquence, southern spokesmen were roused only to anger and bitterness, and reprobated their liberal admirers.

Finally, the full-blown theoreticians of slavery would proudly compare what they saw as the virtues of slavery with what they deemed the cruelty and wretchedness of "white slavery" in England and the American North. The latter worked its hands without stint or mercy, and flung them out to die in the streets or poor-houses when they were no longer of service. They held that the "patriarchal system" of slavery, on the other hand, developed long-term loyalties between servants and masters, ties of love and mutual regard of which commercial civilizations had no understanding. (*See Reading No. 10.*)

CHAPTER 7

Slavery as a "Positive Good"

Reaction Comes to the South. It is possible to pinpoint the time when the southern states committed themselves to a defense of the slavery system (see p. 34). Precisely what factors entered into the decision, however, can never be fully determined. That there were committed reactionaries as far back as slavery's beginnings in America cannot be doubted. Their strength was held in check by others motivated by humanitarian, religious, economic, or other impulses, or by practical situations which impugned the value or the right of slavery. (*See Reading No. 11.*)

Thus, John C. Calhoun, South Carolina statesman and an aspirant to the Presidency, dreamed of a southern industry which would free his section of dependence on manufacturers elsewhere. Prior to the War of 1812, he was a nationalist and expansionist who demanded a high protective tariff on imports, to give native manufacturers an advantage over foreigners. Southern commercial interests, however, failed to rise to the opportunity the war gave them to build industries based on government contracts. Ironically, it was conservative New England businessmen, who had opposed "Mr. Madison's War," believing that it hurt their shipping establishment and made a foe of their traditional friends and customers, Great Britain, who profited by the war. They seized the opportunity it offered and created a new, modern industry in the North.

It is difficult to believe that if a fresh, commercial impulse had swept the South, created urban centers, and demanded skilled workers with incentives to produce competitively, that southern businessmen would have resisted the call for free labor, white and black, at the expense of slaveholders and their ways of life. New southern leaders did not arise. Each year Calhoun grew in his section's esteem. His program changed radically. The nationalist became an intransigent sectionalist. The expansionist became concerned for expansion only when it benefitted slaveholders. Most notoriously, the protectionist became a free-trader, hoping to bargain for better prices among competing manufacturers, domestic and foreign. And the defense of slavery became the cornerstone of Calhoun's master plan and of his followers. (*See Reading No. 12.*)

Free Whites and Free Blacks. The most significant fact about the slaveholder's domain was that it directly affected only about one-fourth of the southern white population. The vast majority of southerners did not own slaves, and had only a tangential economic stake in perpetuating their inferior status. Such stake as a portion of them did maintain was comparable to that of northern poor, notably Irish immigrants driven to the United States by famine at home. They competed with free Negroes for the humbler tasks of the economy. Hatred and derogation became competitive weapons in their hands, particularly tragic because they themselves were targets of suspicion and contempt. "Little southerners" were not above protesting what they deemed an inferior immigration, and believing it better comported with the undiscriminating populations of the North.

Slaveholders who set themselves up as symbols of conduct and achievement to their more modestly endowed fellow citizens could boast of a tradition of democracy which had enabled the children of poor or deteriorated white families to rise by talent and hard work to distinction in law, letters, politics, military affairs, and landownership, and who could claim Patrick Henry and Henry Clay among many others. Jefferson Davis, who became one of the proudest of southern aristocrats, a hero of the Mexican War, and son-in-law of General Zachary Taylor, was born a poor white in Kentucky, in a cabin less than a hundred miles from that of Abraham Lincoln, born the following year. The greater number of non-slaveholders were satisfied to ride second to a brilliant aristocracy, and to define freedom differently for themselves and free Negroes.

The increasingly self-conscious South not only created a folklore of contempt for the Irish and other "alien" stocks of whites. It created a folklore of the plantation, from which even deprived southern whites and the numerous city types from Richmond and Charleston to Memphis and New Orleans·could derive pride and satisfaction.

In such an atmosphere, the status of the free Negro could not improve. The most conspicuous fact respecting his condition was that it was similar both North and South. Universally, he was held to be a "nuisance," who might best be colonized elsewhere, and thus removed, in the North, from a dynamic society. In the South, he constituted an embarrassment to a social compact which tolerated the view, though only part of the white population subscribed to it in theory or practice, that Negroes were legitimately property. Southern laws, as has been seen, were weighted to ensure that the presence of free Negroes did not indirectly impugn this understanding. Southern programs for the free Negroes were not calculated to improve his status or opportunities. (*See Reading No. 13.*)

The Colonization Movement. Organized in 1816 with a host of distinguished northerners and southerners as sponsors, with Federal sanction and philanthropic support, the American Colonization Society was, on the surface, able to answer all questions from every side. Ostensibly, it was intended to offer new opportunities to Negroes, free and enslaved. It would give the former a chance to prove their leadership capacities. It would encourage slaveholders to manumit their slaves in increasing numbers, especially slaveholders fearful of how a skeptical or unsympathetic society would treat their freed men and women. It would unite North and South on the project of dealing positively with their most painful problem. And it would Christianize and civilize the "Dark Continent." It would painlessly undermine the bases of the slave system in the United States. (*See Reading No. 14.*)

Experience demonstrated that the number of manumissions resulting from propaganda favoring colonization, grants, and shipments of Negroes to Liberia was trifling compared with the number of slaves added to the slave population by natural increase. (*See Reading No. 15.*) Moreover, the emphasis of the promoters of colonization, even those patently sincere in their goals, tended to be less upon winning slaveholders over to their banner than to persuade free Negroes to join the exodus from the United States. Negroes' conventions condemned colonization as a blunt effort to uproot and deport them.

James G. Birney, southern aristocrat, became the classic case of a slaveholder who dedicated himself to winning others of his class over to the cause of colonization as a religious and patriotic duty. He found himself shunned and oppressed. His efforts to start a flow of manumissions and emigrations to Africa of freed Negroes was feebly supported and undermanned. His flight, first to Kentucky, a

Border State with little stake in slavery, but where he attracted threats, and then to Cincinnati, Ohio where he was subjected to riots, marked stages in the disillusionment of this first standard-bearer of the Liberty Party in 1840.

Insurrection, Real and Imaginary. Jefferson had romanticized agriculture as embodying human good, as contrasted to commerce and speculation. He did not romanticize slavery, though he himself owned numerous slaves. The abortive effort at revolt in 1800 by a slave, Gabriel, near Richmond, Virginia—not too far from Jefferson's own Monticello—disturbed him and the then-Governor James Monroe. The drastic suppression of the revolt seemed to them to cast shadows on the principles of the Revolutionary War for which they had fought. Nevertheless, they and others held on to the hope that natural processes would erode the institution of slavery which they reluctantly supported.

Events in the South tended to favor slavery, rather than weaken it. The Denmark Vesey "conspiracy" in 1822 was said to have been one of great scope and ingenuity. It did, certainly, deeply involve a former West Indian slave, well-travelled and intelligent, who had bought his freedom and settled in Charleston, S.C. As a result of his exposure, there were sweeping sentences and executions. A Negro Seamen's Act was passed in the state intended to prevent the contamination of slaves by free Negroes abroad. Authorities defied international treaties by removing black sailors from ships entering the Port of Charleston who were citizens not only of Massachusetts, but of Great Britain. These sailors were imprisoned, and even liable to enslavement by sale for costs. In time, these sweeping provisions were copied for use in other southern ports, from Georgia to St. Louis.

Yet it has been denied that there was any substantial evidence at all of a conspiracy, and that "[t]he 'plot' was probably never more than loose talk by aggrieved and embittered men" (Wade, *Slavery in the Cities,* 240–1).

Whatever was the reality of the Vesey affair, there can be no doubt of the fact that it was feared and anticipated, and that the major response of the dominant class was not to redress grievances or seek means for expunging slavery, but of strengthening it through repressive laws and penalties. Much the same could be said of numerous rumors and incidents of alleged plots. That there were slaves of spirit and with ambitions for freedom is evident. Yet as late as the

Civil War it was remarked that with major proportions of armed white men away from home, and with much of the southland defenseless, no significant number of slave rebellions took place. The historian Clement Eaton has suggested that the worst of slavery was not its cruelty toward blacks, but its success in depriving them of the will toward freedom.

The Turning Point for Slavery. However that might be, there can be no questioning the importance, in the gathering social crisis, of the Nat Turner uprising in August of 1831, in a southeastern corner of Virginia. (*See Reading No. 16.*) William Lloyd Garrison had already begun to issue his obscure and meagerly patronized *Liberator* in Boston, when news of the massacre by insurrectionists of fifty-seven white men, women, and children, and the counter-slaughter of the attacking slaves horrified the country. This time, however, demands for security against rebellious slaves were mixed with demands that slavery itself be written off. The Virginia debates in the legislature during its 1831–1832 sessions were fateful to the nation. They were not humanitarian in essence; Negro rights were not at issue. Fearful slaveholders, and resentful, underrepresented poor whites from the hill country opposed slavery and antislavery arguments. The major solution of the antislavery forces was deportation of Negroes from the state.

They failed to carry the legislature. Their collapse signalled not only the collapse of abolitionist possibilities in Virginia, and therefore in the South of which it was the center-piece, but the triumph of the proslavery forces. Thomas R. Dew, a professor at the College of William and Mary, in his *Review* of the Virginia debates (1832) justified slavery in all forms, past and present. His argument became only one of many, clearly and forthrightly asserted, which were in 1852 assembled by dedicated spokesmen as *The Proslavery Argument.* They made Garrison famous or notorious as a mortal enemy of their section, though he repudiated the use of armed force.

Thereafter, proslavery leaders demanded assurances from Washington that their rights in slave property would be kept secure, and their freedom to expand their western holdings respected. (The Missouri Compromise of 1820 had already established a balance of power as between slave states and free.) Manumission societies, which had once seemed a natural efflorescence in the South, it being the locale of slaves, now withered. Thus Levi Coffin, one of a number of North Carolina Quakers who had labored for antislavery measures, found himself so beset by foes as to emigrate with others of his faith and interests to Indiana which, though conservative toward Negroes, permitted them to continue their work.

CHAPTER 8

Slavery as a Way of Life

Southerners and Strangers. More and more the South was perceived as a product of unique circumstances, not only by southerners, but by northern visitors and travellers. Many took the early
viewpoint of the Rev. William Ellery Channing, a founder of Unitar-
ianism who, in youth, spent a year and a half in Richmond, Virginia
as a tutor. His recollections of the South as charming, and as living
by laws different from those governing northern expectations and
society stayed with him many years: indeed until the abolitionist
clamor caused him to review his assumptions.

Before then, many persons of manifest goodwill, even of antislavery goals, but inbred with native traditions of labor and property,
found it easy to accept proslavery understandings of human relations. A curious instance involved a prince of Timbuctoo who became an American slave, whom a series of coincidences made free.
His wife was also freed, for a moderate sum. The case was written by
the Rev. Thomas H. Gallaudet, pioneer reformer in behalf of the
deaf and dumb. He observed that the prince's master "could not rea-
sonably be required to make so great a sacrifice as to set free [the
prince's five sons and eight grandchildren] without a compensation."
At the time of writing (1828), the prince had collected twenty-five
hundred dollars, and needed thirty-five hundred more.

Many others harbored gratifying impressions of the South as
avoiding the bustle and ambition of northern existence, friendly and
courteous in ways unknown to the farmers, merchants, and workingmen of the northern states. They agreed that Negroes were child-
like as a race, happy in their lot, content to sing and serve, and had
limited potential. The Rev. Nehemiah Adams, a Congregational
clergyman of Massachusetts, as late as 1854, could visit the region
and publish *A South-side View of Slavery* which offered essentially a

response similar to Channing's. By that time, abolitionism and events had done their work, and "South-side" Adams had become notorious among derogators of the southern way of life. However, he was far from alone in his opinion.

Thus, the southern mystique was no mere product of southern propaganda, or what came to be known as "southern feeling." It was supported by national tolerance and adaptation to its political goals. The great reversal in attitudes which took place in the 1830's affected reactions to sections and slavery both North and South, and reached Negroes throughout both sections. The daily round of the slaves, in the fields, in the master's house, and in the slave quarters was touched by rumors and ideas about the gathering crisis.

Charles Dickens, visiting the United States in 1842, described mournful aspects of southern civilization as he had seen them in his limited passage through several slave states. (*See Reading No. 17.*) The words of the brilliant, thirty-year-old novelist carried far. Frances Kemble, an English actress married to a southern aristocrat, kept a journal of life on a Georgian plantation in 1838–1839 which, published during Civil War years, was made famous in the North for providing a distressed view of the day-to-day working of slavery. (*See Reading No. 18.*) For example, she not only found repugnant the unwarranted flogging of a female Negro field hand, she also decried the servile flattery and attentions of a quick and intelligent Negro youth, whose understanding of freedom had been reduced (at least on the surface) to a yearning for "massa" to let him keep a pig.

Such incidents, thousands and tens of thousands of times multiplied, became the substance of abolitionist and Free Soil polemics in the 1830–1860 era. They illuminated aspects of a way of life which concerned itself with every detail of existence, ranging from birth to death, the infamy of "breeding" children for the slave market, work, recreation, holidays, clothing, food, friendship, punishment, and religion. All of these aspects of life, and others became pawns of sectional debate. And they utilized the eloquence of free and fugitive Negroes, notably Frederick Douglass, who became a thunderous voice for freedom as in his open letter to his former master, whom he upbraided for personal wrongs and wrongs to his family. He wrote:

> At this moment, you are probably the guilty holder of at least three of my dear sisters, and my only brother in bondage. These you regard as your property. . . . Sir, I desire to know how and where these dear sis-

ters are. Have you sold them? or are they still in your possession. . . .
And my dear old grand-mother, whom you turned out like an old
horse, to die in the woods—is she still alive? . . . Oh! she was to me a
mother, and a father, so far as hard toil for my comfort could make
her such. Send me my grandmother! that I may watch over her and
take care of her in her old age. . . .

Slavery, however, far from reduced its Negro subjects even by
contrast to a silent, anonymous mass. They were known as persons
to their owners, for their physical qualities and intellectual capacities. Within the context of servility, even on the larger plantations,
slaves influenced their workings in every way that personality and
talent could propose. More modestly endowed slaveholders of one
or two servants were likely to be co-workers as much as master and
property. Even "the darker side of slavery"—a side which would be
exploited with every northern nuance of indignation and appeals to
humanity—often involved not agonies and crucifixions, but chagrin
and frustration, often subject to argument and sorting out of issues
and solutions.

Slave Skills in Self-Expression. The mitigating forces within the
slave system are often resented by individuals who demand of students a studied hatred of all that slavery brought about and was.
Certainly, the sunnier aspects of slavery are unfit for the chronicles
of protest. They do, however, help to memorialize the human nature
of the slaves themselves, and the individuality of many of those who
affected southern history. Best known are the slave spirituals: a
major contribution to American lore, and remarkably intertwined
with "white" spirituals, from some of which they frequently derived.
Folktales also furnished a rich source of slave thought and interpretation.

In addition, Negroes developed a wide spectrum of responsiveness
to white community values and concerns. In part, they responded to
dominant social and religious goals, honoring courtship and marriage, religious observances, and standards of social conduct. Where
status and circumstances did not permit full or satisfying compliance
with established custom, slaves deviated from it for their own purposes. Frederick Douglass, in his autobiography, recounted how
overseers resented his independence and dignity and made him
suffer for it. For a time, his despair caused him to join less serious
slave companions in futile carousels. Douglass's forthright character

prevented him from developing devious traits. Others in his situation, including slaves who lived thoughtlessly and without ambition, refined language and other arts for countering authority. (*See Readings Nos. 19 and 20.*)

Major weapons in obtaining material and other ends were deception and passive resistance. Methods of deception were numerous. They included pretending not to understand, direct lying, theft—particularly helpful in augmenting the larder—and layer upon layer of subtle action or pronouncement. Jack Savage, of a Savannah, Georgia plantation, is patently competent, and warrants a high price from a slave-dealer, even though Jack is bitter and rebellious and threatens to run away. He is a bit old for the market. The overseer informs his employer that had Jack been no more than thirty years old, he could have fetched $2500. As it is, he has been sold for $1800. "It would have provoked you," writes the exasperated overseer," to have heard Jack's lies of his inability, &c." Another overseer denounces Negroes as stupid. They cannot realize that if they do not hasten to cut tobacco before the frosts come, the tobacco might be ruined. The Negroes claim they are waiting for the plants to become thicker.

Slaves can threaten their masters in many ways, and they do. They sulk. They warn that they will commit suicide, if they are not given their way. They hide in the thicket, if they have been threatened or abused. Friends or relatives provide them with food and information. A strong chain of slave cooperation will often leave a master or overseer helpless, and glad to come to terms with his recalcitrant slave. Many masters were kindhearted or conscientious, and subject to emotional or intellectual appeals. Others were indifferent, or contemptuous, or malicious. Different tactics and appeals were effective with different personalities, who might include the mistress or daughter of the house, rather than the master. Overseers, too, were of varying quality. A student of the subject concluded "within the limitations imposed by their background . . . , the majority of southern overseers performed their duties with commendable energy, efficiency, and competence" (Scarborough, *The Overseer,* 201).

One Billy Proctor, a Macon, Georgia slave who writes a clear hand and is a house-painter, writes a slaveholder in Americus, also in Georgia, that his master has decided to sell his painters. Proctor is anxious to be purchased by this particular owner. Proctor has excellent recommendations, and can be purchased for $1000—his owner would probably come down fifty dollars:

> Now Mas John, I want to be plain and honest with you. If you will buy me I will pay you $600-per year untill this money is paid, or at any rate will pay for myself in two years. I knew nothing of this matter last night when at your house, or I would have mentioned it while there. I am fearfull that if you do not buy me, there is no telling where I may have to go, and Mr. C. wants me to go where I would be satisfied. . . .

The Domestic Slave-Trade. However roseate might be the advocate or defender of slavery as a just and humane institution, few presumed to portray the traffic in slaves as a happy one. Americans for the most part shut their eyes to the fact that the foreign slave trade, though officially outlawed, persisted, with New York a major port for slavers shipping out with false papers. All this stirred amazement and disbelief when called to public attention.

On the other hand, it was not possible to hide the presence of slave marts in southern and border state towns. From Richmond, Virginia to exotic New Orleans, slaves were congregated for sale under circumstances which, despite commercial blandishments and courtesies, brought out the saddest and most painful aspects of the Negroes' lot, and the least gracious qualities of their captors. Municipal authorities made efforts to control such exhibitions, aware of the demoralizing features of the public slave trade on other slaves, on children, and on others who might react in ways harmful to decency or respect for human nature. The nature of the trade made regulation difficult, and generally ineffective. The barter of human beings, their cattle-like manipulation, and the insensitivity bred in traders by such regular occurrences made them difficult to administer without double standards of civic deportment.

Many travellers and observers noted the "melancholy spectacle" of coffles of slaves, connected with chains, trudging a road on the way to a slave "pen" or mart. In Washington, D.C., such displays became a scandal, one which increasingly outraged visitors from the North, and created the greatest chasm between flag, Capitol, and tradition, and the realities of slavery. Slaves for "breeding," slaves for disposal through trade, slaves subject to the involuntary tearing up of family ties, involuntary lust crystallized attitudes North and South. Such products of the slave trade gave force to opinions that

Negroes were little more than animals, and so not subject to the feelings and conceptions entertained by human beings. They also gave force to the view that the South was no more than a "great brothel" built upon slave labor, mistresses of the great plantation houses no more than "first concubines" in the hierarchy of male-female relations.

Southerners of status themselves expressed distaste for the slave trade and slave traders, and held that they represented an unfortunate side effect of the otherwise admirable southern way of life. It was later one of the brilliant strokes of inspiration in *Uncle Tom's Cabin* which caused Harriet Beecher Stowe to make her plantation owners, Arthur Shelby and Augustine St. Clare, men of sensibility and character. The devilish Simon Legree was New England born and raised. What Mrs. Stowe thus expounded to the nation was the view that individual character, and even sectional character, was not at fault. That it was the system, slavery itself, which created the scenes of intolerable injustice in the South. (*See Reading No. 21.*)

CHAPTER 9

The Challenge of Freedom

Abolitionism and the Slave. William Lloyd Garrison was not the first to preach "immediatism," nor were his views "incendiary" in the sense that he called upon slaves to revolt, or upon fellow-citizens to tear down the slavery establishment with riot and destruction. On the contrary, Garrison opposed all use of "carnal" weapons. The horror and rage which hit upon him as a target, therefore, following the Nat Turner incident, resulted not from any action Garrison or others like him might be expected to undertake. It resulted from fear of an attitude which was not supportive of slavery, and which might therefore unleash impulses within the slavery community disruptive of its operations.

"Gradual" abolitionism had once appeared to be a reasonable viewpoint, to which anyone, including slaveholders, could subscribe. Even Quakers, who had agreed to end slavery entirely within their communities as early as the 1760's, made no effort to foist their views on society at large, and were cold to those Quakers who attempted to do so. Garrison's remarkable achievement was that he made of slavery a moral issue affecting current judgments. He held that there was no difference between those who owned slaves, and those who failed to take a moral stand against slaveholders. Proslavery partisans were perceptive in appreciating that his right to free speech, if sustained by public and legal agencies, would sow seeds of dissatisfaction among thousands of northerners who had previously practiced courtesy toward slaveholders, as fellow-Americans. They had once been content to hope for mild, half-solutions to the dilemmas slavery displayed. Such a stance was especially awkward in a society—on both sides of the Atlantic Ocean—in which free markets and unbound labor was becoming the norm. Garrison's rhetoric of freedom exposed the fact that North and South were going in different directions.

Southern editors often upbraided Garrison for cowardice, in not daring to come below Mason-Dixon with his message, where, of course, he would have been handled very roughly indeed. Garrison's answer to such charges was that his problem was not with the South, but with the North, where "moral pestilence" ruled, and where his message had yet to be appreciated. In fact, he endured riot, ostracism and hatred at home, though he was also able to gather together an inspired and effective following. Garrison's status thus became a barometer of changing attitudes in the North. His program did not actually envision an early end to slavery. He worked unswervingly to establish the view that Americans ought to act *as if* slavery had no claim on their respect. Tactics and strategy calculated to diminish its strength and reach, he thought, would suggest themselves in good time.

Growth of Abolitionist Opinion. The 1830's were the evangelical time of abolition. It succeeded an earnest, but moderate, era of petitions to state assemblies, societies to meliorate the condition of free Negroes, philanthropic groups furthering the education of Negroes and giving aid to runaways north, and manumission societies especially active in border and adjacent states. The new era aroused editors, agitators, and organizers. It raised a host of women who offered moral and material support, from whom a new movement concerned for women's rights would arise. It linked itself with numerous other reforms. These included temperance (actually, prohibition), institutional reform, education, religious inquiry, land reform, and demands for an expanded suffrage. Rhode Island during the "Dorr Rebellion" and New York during the "Anti-Rent" riots experienced what were close to revolutionary outbreaks in behalf of land reform and an enlarged suffrage. The abolitionist impulse gained from all of these concerns, in what was primarily a need for updating old institutions, so that they would prove relevant to new needs and modern circumstances.

The antislavery impulse swept through the North and by 1838 had established some 1350 societies with perhaps two hundred and fifty thousand members and many more sympathizers. The most extraordinary fact respecting this tide of abolitionism was that it did not submerge Garrison. And this despite the sharp or bitter criticism which he attracted from numerous distinguished new leaders of the movement. These included men of the stature of John Greenleaf Whittier, Channing (who in 1835 stirred the country with his *Slavery*, which reversed his earlier opinions), the Tappan brothers, wealthy New York merchants, and many others. They deemed Garrison "excessive" in his criticism of well-intentioned slaveholders, and repellent to hundreds of thousands of American citizens, North and South, who might be willing to help the abolition cause, but who could not tolerate association with Garrison. Evidently, something in Garrison's message and approach made it impossible to forget him.

Was Garrison, and the abolitionist movement, responsible for the new wave of repression which now swept the South? This new wave wholly stopped manumissions, rigidly controlled Negro assemblies, prevented the education of Negroes, and, in addition, censored the United States mails in the South and otherwise defied Federal prerogatives.

It is difficult to determine how much actual harm abolitionist propaganda did to individual Negroes who were at peace with slavery. In addition, national politics became increasingly a skillful, and sometimes desperate arrangement for maintaining the two-party system, above and below Mason-Dixon. However, although Garrison characterized the Constitution as "an agreement with hell," it did include the Bill of Rights, which he was testing in northern precincts. For those Negroes with freedom aspirations, the abolitionist offensive provided new hopes and ideas. There can be no doubt that the undercover arguments and capacities of the Negro communities throughout the nation were multiplied and excited by the abolitionist debate. Precisely how much it increased the incidence of fugitives from slavery can never be known, since most of the facts were of necessity hidden. It is certain, on the other hand, that abolitionists, by aiding and encouraging runaways and exploiting their tales of deprivation and suffering, augmented their numbers and created issues which helped destroy slavery.

The Fugitive Slave. During the 1830–1860 era, fugitive slaves accumulated a literature and lore of their own. Some were famous as cases, rather than individuals. The *Prigg Case* (1842) referred to the attorney for a slave owner, not to Margaret Morgan, a runaway slave who had fled from Maryland to Pennsylvania, and whose forcible return to slavery tested a Pennsylvania law making it illegal to carry a Negro out of the state for purposes of enslavement. The *Latimer Case* of the same year did refer to a runaway slave, George Latimer, seized in Boston for return to Norfolk, Virginia. The case caused severe excitement in Boston, and publication of a daily paper, *The Latimer Journal and North Star*. With Latimer in prison and abolitionists considering desperate actions for freeing him, the owner agreed to payment of four hundred dollars in exchange for dropping his suit.

As noted earlier, the Constitution had provided for the return of fugitive slaves. It had not been specific in describing individual cases and conditions affected, and a national law covering such particulars had been demanded. Such was provided in 1793. This first Fugitive Slave Law was partial to the master; for example, it did not stipulate a trial by jury for alleged runaways. On the other hand, although the law supported the master's right to retrieve a fugitive slave, it placed no significant duties on other citizens to help him in his quest. Over the years this fact caused discontent among slaveholders who had reason to know that northern employers—whether sympathetic to abolition, or not—had been glad to assimilate their runaways into the free labor market. South-side petitions for a stronger fugitive slave law failed, and the issue became part of the developing national debate.

Northern whites had a limited interest in the Negro minority, but they nourished an increasing concern for liberty. Abolitionists publicized the fact that the weak defenses set up for harassed blacks could result in tragedy for whites. A profession of *slave-catchers* had developed which brought to the fore hard and tenacious men, eager to collect rewards, and not too scrupulous about how they might be gained. Certified cases of the kidnapping of free Negroes on the pretext that they were runaways caused unease that the same snare might victimize whites as well, either directly, or because of weakened constitutional safeguards for individuals in general.

Fugitive slaves were mainly a product of the Border States, and contrived to make their way from Maryland and Delaware, Kentucky and Missouri, and also from Virginia. This state not only led into Maryland and Delaware, but also bordered on the Ohio River. Fugitives adopted many modes for finding their way to free states. They followed the North Star. If literate and resourceful, they carried false papers or messages. Sometimes they passed themselves off as free Negroes, or, if complexion permitted, as white. Frederick

Douglass, greatest Negro of his generation, escaped by railroad from Maryland to New York by way of Philadelphia in 1838 by the desperate ruse of utilizing the seaman's papers of a free Negro. Harriet Tubman, "the Moses of her people," not only fled Maryland for Pennsylvania with nothing but wit and steely courage to guide her, but became all but legendary by returning a number of times to lead other slaves out of bondage. Henry "Box" Brown, a Richmond, Virginia slave attained fame by having himself boxed and shipped to Philadelphia. William and Ellen Craft were also nationally known, she of light complexion for having arrayed herself in male attire and passed as a planter, he, the dark-skinned one, for having accompanied her as a body-servant. They made their way through Georgia, South Carolina, Virginia, and Maryland, before reaching Philadelphia and freedom.

And so many others who used opportunity and determination in their bids for freedom. Douglass believed many more could have escaped, had they been willing to leave families and friends without hope of reunion. Some efforts ended in tragedy. Margaret Garner shook the North as much as did any slave when, following her family's flight from Kentucky to Ohio, and their capture, she strove to kill all her children. She did succeed in killing one, before being returned to Kentucky. En route by boat, she attempted suicide with another. She was then sold and lost farther south.

The Underground Railroad. Nevertheless, the effort to prove that slaves did it all: accomplished their own redemption and were the "commanding" force in what came to be known as the Underground Railroad is badly advised and inaccurate. It does not dignify Negro lore, as intended, but merely separates it from the great stream of human American experience which was inevitably dominated by the overwhelming majority of white people, North and South, all of whom, in different groups suffered their own agonies and adjustments and sank them into the American tradition. Slaves by themselves could have done little. It became a major goal of slavery partisans to implicate, by threats or appeals to reason, the entire North in the maintenance of slaveholder's prerogatives. Had this been achieved, the fugitive slave would have become a mere incident in the daily round of the Republic, readily controlled by an effective Fugitive Slave Law.

Dedicated white men throughout the North refused to accept this scheme for ignoring moral issues and brushing off the shadow of civil war which haunted the nation throughout the period. Famous names among aiders and abettors of fugitive slaves emerged to inspire others with their courage and resourcefulness. Rev. Charles T. Torrey, "father of the underground railroad," may have helped some four hundred Negroes to freedom before being apprehended, prosecuted, and committed in 1846 to the penitentiary in Maryland, where he died. Levi Coffin and associates built an elaborate chain of "stations" in Indiana, along which they were able to pass fugitives in transit. Thomas Garrett, a Delaware Friend, was said to have aided more than two thousand seven hundred runaways, though a man of family and wealth, with much to lose. He was candid and notorious in his hatred of slavery and his willingness to service all runaways. Yet Garrett was only caught at his work following years of activity. The severe fine imposed on him was said to have ruined him temporarily; friends and admirers helped him reestablish his business in iron products. Notable was Garrett's declaration in court that he did not intend to stint his duties toward fugitive slaves as he saw it.

Numerous others from Delaware to Illinois and all the way to the Canadian border not only studded the North with "underground stations," but acted directly in bringing slaves out of bondage. Thus Calvin Fairbank, an Oberlin College graduate, and long concerned for fugitive slaves, in 1844 went into Kentucky to bring out the wife of a Negro runaway from slavery. Captured, Fairbank served five years of a jail sentence, and, pardoned, returned to his work. He was again seized, this time in Indiana, and returned to prison in Kentucky, not to emerge again until 1864.

Although all Negroes, free or slave, were far from committed to freedom enterprises any more than all whites were, and though northern and southern Negro communities harbored predictable assortments of lightminded elements and "Judases" capable of informing on fugitives and alleged fugitives, there were certainly strong currents among Negroes which gave them power in fugitive slave operations. They harbored fugitives, moved them East, West, and North to friends, raised money for them, and performed many other services of mercy and affection. Alone, however, they could have accomplished only a tithe of the "underground" work which was actually performed. And the effort to publicize and develop this work —to implicate skeptics in it on grounds of humanity, and to bring out the moral meaning of the underground railroad, particularly important because it transgressed the law of the land—could only be

done by white orators, clergymen, and others who could not be ignored by their families and associates, their audiences and their con-
gregations. Frederick Douglass was one of the greatest of abolitionist spokesmen, but, alone, he would have had no voice. William Still,
a distinguished Philadelphia Negro, who later prepared one of the
vital chronicles of northern labors for fugitive slaves, *The Underground Railroad* (1873) never thought to do anything but honor his
white coadjutors. His indispensable book (along with Wilbur H. Sie-
bert's masterly *The Underground Railroad from Slavery to Freedom*
[1899]) is a monument of tribute to white heroes and heroines as well
as to his own people.

The Border States and Slavery. The Border States were early
recognized as containing the key to the future of slavery. They could
act as a buffer for slavery, or militate against its inner security or
spread. Set beside the free states, the Border States were influenced
by their presence, and, in Maryland and Delaware, by their direct
contiguity. The Ohio and Mississippi Rivers gave Kentucky and
Missouri an element of remoteness from the free states on the other
side, but boats and travellers reduced their privacy considerably.

All the Border States offered apparent advantages to slaves. Although Frederick Douglass despised slavery as much in Baltimore as
out of it, he did agree that its Negroes esteemed themselves as more
consequential than "the whip-driven slaves on the plantation." Ken-
tuckians prided themselves on their pioneer heritage and were not
impressed by pieties respecting the virtues of slavery. Many of their
kin had emigrated to Missouri, and set up plantations along the Missouri River, weaving through the state and uniting St. Louis and
Kansas. (*See Reading No. 22.*) Here slavery tended toward the patriarchal ideal. However, the growth of St. Louis, attracting German
immigrants fiercely antagonistic toward slavery, created a division of
opinion which would later affect the fortunes of war. Slavery did
maintain its establishment in St. Louis, and with substantial public
support. There, indeed, one of the horrendous events of slavery took
place, in 1836, when a mulatto sailor was burned alive by a mob.
This event gave rise to the curious doctrine of a local judge that,
though such an atrocity could be accounted a crime when perpetra-
ted by one or two persons, it became defensible when it was en-
dorsed by many persons in the form of a mob.

Lincoln in his great debates with Stephen A. Douglas made it a
point of distinction between them that his opponent was unwilling to

find differences between slavery and freedom. Lincoln was intensely the heir of poor whites and English ancestors. He had no great feelings for Negroes, but he had every concern for ideals of freedom and tangibles of independence. His problem with slavery was that of many persons in the Border States who owned and wished to own no slaves: their respect for those who did, for constitutional compromises, and for the laws of property.

All the Border States gave rise to antislavery and even abolitionist opinions, but Kentucky produced Cassius M. Clay, the son of slaveholders, who was persuaded that he would rise in national affairs by leading Kentucky out of slavery. He defended his program with guns and bowie knives: a spectacle which deluded northern partisans into imagining that slavery would fall of itself, at least in the Upper South. The pride, however, which Border State slaveholders took in their more "humane" versions of slave relations—an opinion which was not shared by their Deep South brethren—and the disgust which they expressed over slave-dealers and their enterprises seem to have accomplished little more than to ensure that civil strife, if it came, would be particularly bitter and desperate, as brother turned on brother in border wars.

Search for a Solution. Slaves made their greatest contribution to the national debate as fugitives. As objects of pity or contempt, as narrators interpreting slavery to the nation, and as individuals raising constitutional questions which challenged the legal foundations of the American system, they stirred friends and enemies. Daniel O'Connell, "The Liberator," leader in Ireland's fight for independence from Great Britain, joined others among his people to issue a manifesto condemning American slavery. On the other hand, Irish in America received with acclaim John Mitchel, a hero of Irish resistance, who escaped transportation to come to the United States, where he announced himself to be proslavery. "[W]e, for our part," he wrote grimly, in response to the strictures of a benevolent Irish gentleman and abolitionist, James Houghton, "wish we had a good plantation, well-stocked with healthy negroes [sic], in Alabama." Mitchel later served the Confederacy as journalist and editor.

The program of the proslavery South was wide and much encompassing. Thomas Jefferson, in old age, had suggested that it would dampen prospects for civil war and also ameliorate the lot of Negroes to nationalize slavery, by permitting slaves to be carried and worked anywhere in the states. His plan had been patriotically intentioned. He had been frightened for the country's safety by the uproar in 1820 over Missouri's entrance into the Union as a slave state. And he was benevolent in his view of slaves. One of his own, Isaac, later dictated a memoir describing the pleasant round of life on Jefferson's Monticello estate.

The new proslavery attitude which succeeded Jefferson's was sectional, and intended to secure and expand slavery. (*See Reading No. 23.*) It treated the Federal Union as secondary to its own "sovereignty," remembering the Revolution as legitimately separatist. To the extent that "British gold" helped subsidize abolition in America, it despised philanthropy from abroad. It was, however, gratified when Thomas Carlyle, one of the greatest living names in British letters, in his enthusiasm for great men and hard work, offered an "Occasional Discourse on the Nigger Question" (1849) in terms which outraged abolitionists on both sides of the water.

Above all, proslavery defenders repeated in ever-heightening pitch, that slavery offered more to an inevitable labor force than did the "freedom" of the Industrial Revolution. They cited with satisfaction the findings of Parliamentary hearings which detailed the somber, hopeless lot of women, children, and men in the mines and mills. (*See Reading No. 24.*) They gave less regard to the labors of such reformers as the Seventh Earl of Shaftesbury, who forced through the hearings in the first place, abolished the sad trade of "Climbing Boys" (chimney-sweeps), established his famous Ragged Schools, and instituted systems of government inspection and control in almost every field of work: systems which gained strength with labor education and organization.*

Northern Responses. It was even held by critics of abolitionism that philanthropists emphasized the problem of enslavement at the expense of larger social and economic needs which affected the great majorities. Negroes, after all, constituted only some ten percent of the population. Nevertheless, it seemed impossible to stem the current of unrest respecting slavery. Followers of Andrew Jackson had argued that abolition was a "conservative" movement, diverting attention from a "radical" national program which had included at-

* Ronald T. Takaki, *A Pro-Slavery Crusade: The Agitation to Reopen the African Slave Trade* (New York, 1971) examines personalities who rationalized the justice and desirability of slavery on moral and material grounds.

tacks on the Second Bank of the United States and also battles on behalf of President Martin Van Buren's Independent Treasury scheme, which enabled the government to retain its own funds. Abolitionists maintained that so long as property rights in human beings were countenanced, individual rights could not be advanced.

The program fostered by the abolitionists themselves ranged from the moral argument, as enunciated by the "immediatists," with attendant action on behalf of slaves, to the efforts of "political abolitionists" who hoped to win over the nation—or at least, the northern part of the nation—at the polls. Their Liberty Party in 1840 made almost no impression in an election which highlighted the picturesque Whig campaign promoting "Tippicanoe and Tyler, too." The Liberty Party's seven thousand, one hundred votes in that year seemed pitiable. Four years later, however, the country rang with the sensation it created, when its fifteen thousand, eight hundred twelve votes in New York State lost Henry Clay the Presidency. Thereafter, no politician could ignore the slavery issue, though his tactics for meeting it varied with individuals. (*See Reading No. 25.*)

The North Chooses Freedom. By 1850, continuous quarrels over fugitive slaves, the role of Texas in the Union, petitions for ending slavery in the District of Columbia, and other troublesome dilemmas had created a public mood which sent politicians out seeking to control the overriding issue of slavery once and for all. Most momentous seemed the question of new territories in the West, which both southern and northern statesmen studied anxiously, in formulating their approaches. In 1850, Henry Clay made his final effort to create a program to which the entire country could subscribe. His Compromise of that year had many features intended to placate all the major factions. Its most exciting aspect, however, was the Fugitive Slave Act which, in effect, sought to stop the disruptions of law and tranquillity which fugitives inspired. The Act bound all marshals and deputy marshals everywhere "to obey and execute all warrants and precepts issued under the provisions of this act, when to them directed." In a word, the Act would have forced civil authorities to capture and return runaways, and, in addition, it would have mobilized "all good citizens . . . to aid and assist in the prompt and efficient execution of this law." (*See Reading No. 26.*)

The North rose in protest against it. It was actually enforced, under President Franklin Pierce, when in 1854 the runaway Anthony Burns was seized in Boston and prepared for return. Abolitionists and their sympathizers condemned the deed and its administrators in unrestrained terms and sought to tear Burns away from his jailors. In the course of the action, one of them was shot and killed. Troops lined the street from the courthouse to the wharf, as Burns was put on ship before twenty thousand excited Bostonians. It was a painful and expensive victory for the government. Each succeeding "rendition" of fugitives sank its prestige still further. For general purposes, the law was dead.*

These developments were viewed with intensive care by the brilliant proslavery writer George Fitzhugh of Virginia, a pioneer sociologist, a close student and correspondent of the abolitionists, who even delivered a lecture on "The Failure of Free Society" at the New Haven (Conn.) Lyceum. Fitzhugh was convinced that the nation would finally have to agree that it was proceeding on false principles. He would not accept as accurate the statement in the Declaration of Independence that governments "derive their just powers from the consent of the governed." The women, the children, the Negroes had not been consulted in the Revolution, he asserted. Few of the nonproperty holders had been. The truth was that the Founding Fathers had been despots. All effective governments had to be composed of despots. Fitzhugh wrote:

> The Social Revolution now going on at the North, must some day go backwards. Shall it do so now, ere it has perpetrated an infinitude of mischief, shed oceans of blood, and occasioned endless human misery; or will the Conservatives of the North let it run the length of its leather, inflict all these evils, and then rectify itself by issuing into military despotism?

Fitzhugh's own solution, in his *Cannibals All!* (1857), was an alliance between conservative southerners and northerners who would agree on both slavery and control of the many voices north asserting their natural rights, in and out of law. But northerners, conservative and otherwise, rejected despotism as a solution to the nation's agony. Their enthusiasm and support enabled them to win Kansas as a free state. This was a remarkable achievement, since proslavery forces received help from slaveholders in adjacent Missouri, and

---

* However, see Stanley W. Campbell, *The Slave-Catchers: Enforcement of the Fugitive Slave Law 1850–1860* (Chapel Hill, 1970), for details of its later career.

also from the Federal government itself, which attempted to force a proslavery constitution upon the Territory. Northerners made a hero of John Brown, even though he was committed to "meddling" with slavery as an institution: a policy which ensured civil war.

The subtle logic which guided the North's decisions can be observed in the "Free Kansas" slogans, which rejected statehood with slavery, but won it under a state constitution which gave the right to vote only to white males. Northerners valued their prejudices. They valued their families and communities. Consciously or unconsciously, black and white, they valued their traditions. But they resented Federal pressures which would have deprived them of their local autonomy. And for the principles of the Declaration of Independence, which they esteemed as their common heritage, they ultimately revealed themselves as being ready to lay down their lives.

CHAPTER **10**

The Verdict of War

Slavery in the Balance. Southern intellectuals employed every argument to justify secession. They held that Lincoln's election to the Presidency was a sectional victory. Lincoln's program for restricting the territorial enlargement of slavery meant to them the abrogation of the Federal "compact." A few insisted that they were defending freedom—some even free trade—rather than slavery, as their forefathers had done during the Revolution. A few released their slaves in order to enter into the struggle uncompromised. The majority of southerners, however, accepted the view that it was slavery itself which was being justified and defended, and in its behalf put resourceful commanders and courageous troops in the field to resist Federal authority. (*See Reading No. 27.*)

Lincoln, on taking office, had appealed to southern loyalty, and offered to enforce the Fugitive Slave Law, if doing so would prevent secession. Such moderate statements enraged northern radicals. They did not, however, face the problem with which Lincoln coped. It was his task to hold together a divided North, ranging from Free Soil and abolitionist Massachusetts to Ohio and Indiana, which harbored proslavery and antislavery elements in confused abundance. Lincoln's main political goal throughout his administration was to keep the Border States from seceding, since with them lay the future of the Union. Northern armies needed to *defeat* the Confederacy. The South needed only to attain a *stalemate* in order to win independence. With the Border States gone, a stalemate could not have been avoided. A stabilized and recognized Confederacy would have contained its slaves with border guards and a trained constabulary, and riveted slavery on Negroes in the South for the foreseeable future.

Therefore, although Lincoln found slavery repugnant and cher-

ished hopes for its eventual decline, he avoided all actions or statements which might turn unionists in the Border States against the
Federal government. He would not permit the official use of Negroes
in Federal army units, a policy frustrating to free Negroes eager to
join in overthrowing the slave South, and to prove their character as
deserving of national respect. Nor would Lincoln at first approve actions of commanders who wished to free slaves in territory which
they had overrun.

Role of Free and Enslaved Negroes. The distinguished role of
free Negroes during the war has been amply spelled out. They
sought and took advantage of all opportunities to serve, and to dignify their military and civilian circumstances. Frederick Douglass
set the tone here as elsewhere for his people, resisting, among other
things, a feeling among some of them that this was a "white man's
war":

> Once let the black man get upon his person the brass letters U.S.;
> let him get an eagle on his button and a musket on his shoulder, and
> bullets in his pocket, and there is no power on earth or under earth
> which can deny that he has earned the right to citizenship in the
> United States. I say again, this is our chance, and woe betide us if we
> fail to embrace it.

Indeed, there were many powers competent to deny aspects of
Douglass's dream. The war tested all of them. The government, for
propaganda purposes, assumed a moral stance against the enemy,
caricaturing him as a Lord of the Lash. It actually, in 1862, hanged a
slave trader for "piracy on the high seas." But Congress linked military goals with expedience, in its policies toward Negroes. Thus, its
Confiscation Act in 1861 denied the right of owners to slaves being
used for purposes of rebellion, as in the building of fortifications.
The Act struck at southern military measures, rather than at slavery.
When General John C. Frémont, as commander of the Western Department of the Union Army, that same year proclaimed the slaves
of rebels in his Department free, Lincoln hastened to abrogate the
order. It went too far beyond the Confiscation Act, he believed. It
especially endangered Federal hopes for keeping Missouri from falling to Confederate forces. Also set aside was General David Hunter's later Order (May 9, 1862) announcing martial law in the Military Department of the South (Georgia, South Carolina, and
Florida), and "freeing" the slaves of the area: an Order which
Hunter could not have significantly implemented.

Meanwhile, Negroes served in the hundreds of thousands, North and South, in camps and in industry, as free men and as slaves. For the northern commanders, they spied and carried messages; Harriet Tubman and Sojourner Truth were only two among many who contributed in these vital capacities. Some Negroes also served in military capacities thanks to the enterprise of individual commanders, acting without government sanction. In the North, too, the great turning point for Negroes was the Enrollment Act of March 3, 1863, which was interpreted as permitting the enlistment of free Negroes. A Bureau of Colored Troops was established to systematize the work. Black regiments were raised which performed outstandingly in such actions as that at Fort Wagner, near Charleston, South Carolina, July 16, 1863. The next year occurred the battle at Fort Pillow, on the Mississippi, which was held by Union troops, about half of whom were Negroes. The engagement became notorious because of the ruthless killing of Federal troops who were seeking to surrender, once the Fort had been breeched. The Confederate defense against accusations of slaughter was that the troops had fought fiercely, and required killing in order to be suppressed. There can be little doubt that it was the presence of the Negro portion of the troops which was responsible for the sorry event.

The progress of Negro service with the military in the South was even more rapid, though Lincoln had feared charges that he might be arming insurrectionists. The record of slaves during the long hostilities was mixed. An interesting hypothesis has held that the most spirited slaves sought and found every opportunity to join or accompany Union forces, thus depriving the great majority of slaves of their natural leadership. Nevertheless, some slaves did offer Federal commanders their knowledge and sinews, and both were solicited by unionists. The overwhelming number of slaves were utilized, by both northern and southern leaders, as laborers and skilled workers. For the most part slaves neither aspired to nor were seriously considered by Confederates for military service proper.

The situation was more complicated between slaves and Union elements. In general, slaves responded positively to freedom and the hope of freedom. Precisely how aggressive they were in plotting insurrections, engaging in arson, and otherwise waging war on their masters must always be a matter of partial conjecture. Rumor and fact were, as before the war, intermingled. Even lynchings and executions were not always certain evidence of matured and widespread plots. A milestone was, however, early achieved in May of 1861, when three runaways presented themselves at Fortress Monroe, Virginia, which was in Union hands. General Benjamin F. Butler, in command, refused to release them to their owner, arguing that they had been utilized for rebellious purposes, having been employed in the construction of Confederate military works. Hence, said Butler, they were "contraband of war." Thereafter, hundreds of runaways fled to the fortress, and were eagerly used in numerous capacities, in some cases having to do with actual war conduct. While arguments raged over the arming of Negroes, the Navy followed an established peacetime tradition by accepting Negroes for service on ship. Relatively little distinction was made regarding their missions, except that they were given inferior technical ratings.

The "contraband of war" formula employed thousands of Negroes along the Atlantic coast, and at such key points as New Orleans and Vicksburg on the Mississippi River. The effectiveness of slaves for war service could be measured by the Confederate War Department order of April 21, 1862, which sought to categorize their white officers as felons and slave-stealers, subject to execution. The War Department in Washington was prompt to threaten retaliation, if any captured soldier should be executed on such pretexts. The Confederate order was not implemented.

Doubtless in the largest sense, Negroes, whether free or enslaved, were inadequately used by the Union strategists. But considering the fearful stakes of victory and defeat, the best policy, if not the most virtuous, is difficult to assess. Nor was public opinion dependable in the crisis. Thus General Butler, mentioned above, was a "political general," one of the numerous politicians Lincoln was forced to honor even though they had not commanded troops, or even, in Butler's case, worn a uniform. Yet these "political generals" held their troops' lives in their hands. Butler's acceptance in Virginia of runaways, and his "contraband" formula gave him an amazing popularity in the North. So popular was he that he may have turned down an offer by Lincoln to become his vice-presidential candidate for a second term. Butler imagined he would succeed Lincoln in 1864 as President on his own political merits.

Yet Butler was a notorious opportunist who, in any greater capacity than he enjoyed, could have severely harmed the Federal program. As it was, his popularity no more than revealed an emotional, simplistic view of the conflict; one which added to Lincoln's burdens, but which did not deter him from his task. This mainly added up to marshalling the North's superior resources in material and manpower, and applying pressure upon southern commanders until they could be persuaded to surrender.

That the war also gave vent to a great deal of sacrifice and idealism cannot be doubted. Colonel Robert Gould Shaw, who died with the Negroes of the 54th Massachusetts Regiment in the assault on Fort Wagner, and Colonel Thomas Wentworth Higginson, also of Massachusetts, who led the First South Carolina Volunteers, have been recently accused of patronizing their Negro troops. This they may have done in some intrinsic sense. How much this impugns the imperial dignity of their effort and concern is debatable. It suffices here to note that the same public which made a fad of Butler and his "contrabands" made hard the task of those who sought to employ Negroes in the full prosecution of the war. How appropriate are the slogans of a later generation to the circumstances of an earlier one always bears analysis.

The Crumbling of the Slavery System. During the early stages of the war, slavery as a viable system of civilization seemed under stress only to the extent that the northern effort required a strong propaganda effort which held slavery and its supporters up to scorn. As late as October 7, 1862, Gladstone, pride of English Liberals, expressed the view that: "[T]here is no doubt that Jefferson Davis and other leaders of the South have made an army; they are making, it appears, a navy; and they have made what is more than either, they have made a nation." Thus, English abolitionism was earnest and vocal, but far from dominating English opinion. The French, though they had emancipated their own colonial slaves in 1849, watched and waited throughout the Civil War, in imitation of the British. And so did other nations, ready to accept or reject the Confederacy according to the fortunes of war.

Hence, often reiterated fears of unleashed Negro slaves, the fearsome Draft Riots in New York City in July of 1863 which cost, among other effects, the lives of helpless Negroes and even the sacking and burning of an orphanage for Negro children—these and other events bespeaking antipathy for blacks gave no promise that slavery need necessarily disappear as a result of the war. The furor caused by the Emancipation Proclamation, though it officially freed no slaves, and the fact that the Fugitive Slave Law was still on the books, though little honored, helped indicate the jeopardy in which concepts of freedom continued to stand. All such facts gave added point to Lincoln's emphasis, in his Second Inaugural Address, on "[t]he progress of our arms, upon which all else chiefly depends." (*See Reading No. 28.*)

Gettysburg was not only the last great effort of the Confederacy. It was its last great effort to split the Union, and it all but did so. Thereafter, the Confederates massed to take the shock of northern military power—including Negro regiments which added up to some one hundred, eighty thousand troops—and to hope for a moderate northern view of its social system. General Ulysses S. Grant's ruthless assault on Confederate lines in Virginia cost the North dearly in human lives, but it also bled the Confederacy, driving it at last to tolerate the idea of arming its slaves. The protest by Howell Cobb of Georgia, that "[i]f slaves can make good soldiers, our whole theory of slavery is wrong," indicated to what straits his generation had been driven.

The break up of the Confederate government, and General Robert E. Lee's surrender at Appomattox, therefore, seemed not only the defeat of rebellion, but the death of slavery. As William Lloyd Garrison said, having travelled with a party by boat to Charleston, South Carolina, in that Jubilee year, and having laid his hand on the monument to John C. Calhoun: "Down into a deeper grave than this slavery has gone, and for it there is no resurrection."

CHAPTER 11

The Continuing Debate

Reconstruction and Freedom. The end of the war released high hopes that the moral issues which had plagued the entire nation had been settled. The Thirteenth Amendment to the Constitution, prohibiting "involuntary servitude, except as a punishment for crime whereof the party shall have been duly convicted" was not contested by the defeated South. It was the Fourteenth Amendment, apparently protecting the civil rights of Negro Americans, and the Fifteenth Amendment, granting the vote to Negro males—these were the protested Amendments. Believing that they raised questions of a different order from those involving slavery, William Lloyd Garrison closed down his *Liberator*, considering that its mission had been accomplished.

With Federal troops parading the southern states, Negroes emerged in the South who were able to assume the varied roles of citizens, including that of legislator. The Freedmen's Bureau undertook to acclimate less talented former slaves to conditions of liberty, and to help educate as well as feed them in their new circumstances. New *Black Codes*, intended to control the Negroes' privileges, were formulated by southern whites seeking to reassert their supremacy in the new social order. The Codes were formally suspended by Federal military governors, but the "prostrate South" found informal means for curbing the aspirations of Negroes. Most notorious was the first Ku Klux Klan, founded in 1866 and publicly disbanded three years later. Despite Federal acts intended to destroy such organizations, states-rights court interpretations and diminished northern concern for the freedmen enabled southern whites committed to separate and unequal doctrines of race relations to continue their struggle for dominance. (*See Reading No. 29.*)

"Wage Slavery." In the meantime, Wendell Phillips, second only to Garrison in the antislavery crusade, and the nation's greatest living orator had discovered a new cause. Slavery, he agreed, was dead (though, unlike Garrison, he felt compelled to fight for the freedmen's Amendments as a necessary adjunct to the great battle). But *wage slavery* was more virulent than ever before. Not only had northern opinions triumphed. Northern industry had exploded into maturity, thanks to war incentives, and at the expense of the labor it employed. Its use of Chinese labor, for example, had produced unrest and riots, instigated by resentful white workingmen, in the West. Especially harmful to American labor's living standards and hopes was the system of *contract labor* which, in post-Civil War years, enabled employers to bring in workers from abroad on terms which stipulated twelve-months labor in exchange for payment of the immigrant's passage. Here was a modern version of the old colonial "redemptioner" labor system. Although this means for acquiring cheap labor was legally ended by the *Contract Labor Act* of 1885, a new, resourceful industry continued to find ways for keeping labor abundant and cheap. It occupied factories in the burgeoning cities and raised entire mill-towns in the countryside. To work its mines and machines it attracted and encouraged vast streams of a *new immigration,* composed of eastern and southern European peasant peoples. Their lives quickly sank into tragedy and disorder in overcrowded tenements and heavily policed company premises.

The "New South." Reconstruction proper ended as a result of the "Disputed Election" of 1876, which left the country dangerously without a duly-elected President. As the result of a political compromise, painfully arranged by means of an informally constituted "Electoral Commission," the Republican candidate Rutherford B. Hayes received the Presidency on the understanding that Federal forces would be removed from the southern states. Hayes implemented that understanding. His order withdrawing the troops capped a long series of retreats by Federal agents before determined southern white leaders, and effectively returned control of the southern states to them. (*See Reading No. 30.*) A new breed, they professed to speak aggressively for the *poor whites,* whom they declared had been betrayed by the erstwhile plantation aristocrats. Ben Tillman of South Carolina was typical of this new leadership which scorned the sentimentalities of slavery, demanded economic and social reforms for the poor, and was equally vigorous and uncompromising in withholding equal rights from Negroes.

George W. Cable (1844–1925), a loyal southerner who loved his native Louisiana, held that in order to hold the Negro down it was necessary for his own people to get down in the gutter with him. Accordingly, Cable denounced a social system which was not only harsh and unjust to Negroes, but to poor whites as well. This system posited *sharecrop, tenant-lease,* and *crop-lien* arrangements calculated to hold the average worker on the land perpetually responsible or in debt to the landowner or those who furnished seed and provisions. It was a system backed by a rigid convict and jail program and convict-labor contracts which had few reform or correctional features. They were notorious in their ability to harden and embitter their white victims as well as their black. Critics of these new social procedures and the police machinery accompanying them held that they were as repressive as—perhaps more repressive than—the slavery system they had superseded. Cable, a sensitive literary artist as well as a social critic, set down his views memorably in *The Silent South* (1885). As a result he found it necessary to leave his homeland and take up new residence in the North.

Whether, then, southern whites had succeeded in nullifying the results of civil war and reestablished their former estate, modernized for new conditions, seemed a matter of interpretation. It had to take into account the fact that, as northern white labor found ways to improve its status and prospects through unions, reform movements, and political maneuvers, so southern freedmen and their families found ways to ameliorate their lot and advance their hopes. A major tragedy in their affairs was the career of Thomas E. Watson of Georgia, a vibrant young white idealist who at first held that the rich oppressed the poor, black and white. As a Populist in the 1890's, Watson sought a black-white alliance against monopolistic and other oppressive forces. While his program deteriorated into venomous hatred of Negroes and others he deemed harmful to the "people," he continued to the end to rage against the evils of wealth in ways which maintained for him the admiration of many leaders of reform.

Numerous whites everywhere in the nation were unwilling to concede that Negroes required special consideration—that the status of Negroes differed in essence from that of such other troubled categories as Indians, unassimilated immigrants, children of the poor, the aged, working women, and others harassed by social competition and indifference. Also, such a Negro leader as Booker T. Washington, born in slavery and the head of Tuskegee Institute, rejected the view that he was enmeshed in a new slavery. In his landmark Atlanta (Georgia) Exposition Address (1895), Washington emphasized that it was vastly more important for his own people to be prepared to exercise the privileges of the law, than to have those privileges. He recalled with pride the record of Negro loyalty and its material contribution to the South. In his address's most famous passage, he asserted: "In all things that are purely social we can be as separate as the fingers, yet one as the hand in all things essential to mutual progress."

Such sentiments were infuriating to spirited geniuses of his race, among whom W. E. B. Du Bois was preeminent. There were, however, comparable differences of viewpoint among other peoples and groups. Daniel De Leon and "Big Bill" Haywood, labor radicals, were extreme in their derogation of Samuel Gompers, founder and reigning leader of the American Federation of Labor. They held he was a betrayer of workingmen, rather than a builder in their behalf, and they compared the portion of many workers with that of slaves. Charlotte Perkins Stetson was one of many talented females who were oppressed by a sense of enslavement in a male world. She, and others like her, took little pride in the arts and social graces which made life worthwhile to great numbers of "dependent" women.

"White Slavery." A related concept from the past persisted in the association of "white slavery" with prostitution. Although Negro women were also employed in this pursuit, and as a rule were subject to the will of male masters, the greater percentage of white females so bound permitted them to be identified with the term. It was also used to designate the international trade in women. In due time it concerned international commissions seeking to curb female exploitation, involuntary servitude, the spread of sexual diseases, and other aspects of the "white slave" traffic.

Negro and Immigrant Compared. A proper assessment of American social conditions as they affected native Negroes would, as in the past, demand that they be contrasted to those of others harassed by alien and unfriendly conditions in a social order which emphasized free enterprise's rewards and penalties. Slavery as a social system, defended and defined by law, tradition, and expectation had been effectively outlawed in the United States.* But southern ways

* It should be noted that, from time to time, individual cases of servitude, and even group relations which seemed to infringe upon the Thir-

continued to diverge from northern ways. Thus, William Still, as a Philadelphian, found himself subjected to segregation in the newly developed and instituted streetcars of that city. He fought successfully to obtain equal rights in public conveyances for himself and his people: a victory which was not to be secured in his generation by his brethren farther south.

Nevertheless, they, too, struggled for status and emoluments and joined many of their social labors to those of Negroes in the North. August Meier's *Negro Thought in America, 1880–1915* (1963) indicates that leaders of the Negro community never flagged in their efforts to strengthen unity and effectiveness. Their debates, conventions, and organizational efforts do not suggest conditions of slavery, or even of peonage. They tally to a considerable degree with similar efforts undertaken by beset and disillusioned immigrant groups— lacking roots and traditions in America, and even the native tongue —who constantly lost their most adroit and talented elements to the general population. The stigma of color and "previous condition of servitude" still distinguished many Negroes, in a nation of people who could forget or ignore their own previous conditions of indentureship. They also did not hesitate to discriminate against newer white immigrants, assign derogatory terms to them, and generalize that they were "slave-minded" and of inferior "stock."

However, it has been argued that the fact of color distinguished the plight of the Negro from that of the white immigrant, who could advance in social status as he advanced economically. The Negro could not do so, it is alleged. Economic improvements, in the case of Negroes, did not lead to social improvements. Whatever the facts might be on the higher levels of intellectuality and affluence among Negroes, it seemed to angry libertarians that the mass of American Negroes endured a condition which was "close" to slavery. A responsible concern for this vital challenge requires a comparative look at social conditions as they affected Negroes and others elsewhere.

Slavery, and Permutations of Slavery. Slavery continued to be a living institution in many parts of the world. In Africa, the exploration and settlement of new areas by white people continued in the

---

teenth Amendment, came to public attention. They always appeared as curious deviations from accepted social standards, offering no responsible challenge to them.

post-Civil War era. These activities focussed new attention on Africa and its native peoples, and a fresh awareness of the slave-trade and domestic slave practices as they affected large African areas north and south. The Indian Ocean and the Red Sea became notorious as means for transporting slaves beyond the "dark" continent. Although the facts were known and repeated, no great antislavery movement resulted in the United States among Negroes or whites. (English philanthropists did maintain an antislavery testimony.)

Yet the conscience of Europe was disturbed. For example, the signatories to the treaty drawn up by the Brussels Conference on slavery of 1890 pledged themselves to give mutual aid in curbing the slave trade, along with related trades in guns and liquor. Little progress resulted. The reasons appear to have been the same as those which kept slavery alive and vigorous in such disparate parts of the world as China, India, the Philippines, and large areas of South America. Various forms of slavery were profitable. And since they derived from long established modes of life and religion, there was little direct incentive for abolishing them. In addition, they varied so widely in forms as to confuse issues of what, precisely, ought to be abolished, in a world which required laborers. Various conventions resulted in the formal "abolition" of slavery in a number of countries, and the avowals of governments that they would intercept slave traders and subject them to punishment. But such simple solutions did not solve the problem of distinguishing between slavery and debt-bondage, serfdom (or peonage), the practice of selling women which had to be in some fashion distinguished from tribal dowry and other marriage customs, "adoptions" of children which were in reality purchases, forced labor which could be defended on numerous domestic and international grounds, among other matters of policy and practice.

One of many examples was furnished by Egypt, where English overseers, honoring their now-established antislavery policies, struggled to cope with the implications of such distinctions as those separating white Circassian and darker Abyssinian slaves, on the one hand, and black slaves from Nubia, Kordfan, and Darfour. All these and other human beings were subject to their master's preferences, duties, and expectations. And though these masters gave more status, for various reasons, to one type of female over another, and to males of different characteristics, they were all, nevertheless, subject to conditions which could only be termed slavery. Observers discriminated between such elements of Egypt's subordinate people and its long established communities of technically more free fella-hin. A more pertinacious view of their circumstances sees them as possibly inferior, in some respects to those of some categories of Egyptian slaves, and patently lower in degree to that of all but the meanest of erstwhile American slaves, whom they preceded and fol-lowed in time:

> As they were under the Pharaohs, the Ptolemies, the Romans, and the Caliphs, so in the main are they now—the most patient, the most pacific, the most home-loving, and withal the merriest race in the world. In this latter respect the oppression of more than forty centu-ries has failed to dampen their natural buoyancy of spirit; and no-where more than amid the mud huts and seemingly abject poverty of a fellah village does "the human heart vindicate its strong right to be glad." *

This observer believed that Egyptian slavery, though subject to cruel tribal wars, kidnappings, and barbaric practices was, once stabilized, "simply domestic servitude under practically efficient guarantees against ill-treatment." So, with variations, said travellers among other slave-supporting nations, though all agreed that slavery was an out-moded system and "must perforce die out" with time. They also took curious satisfaction in contrasting the humanity they discerned in such slavery systems as the above and what they saw as the atrocious quality of slavery in the United States, as drawn in *Uncle Tom's Cabin.*

Slavery as a Continuing Factor in Social Thought and International Affairs. Slavery without qualification or concern for public opinion, nevertheless, continued to manifest itself. As an example, the Queensland sugar plantation, during the last quarter of the nineteenth century, utilized labor kidnapped from the Polynesian islands. Outraged public opinion in Great Britain brought some changes in the Australian labor system by the end of the century, but comparable circumstances elsewhere continued to embarrass diplomats and trouble the consciences of reformers. The League of Nations took the subject into its purview. Its experts offered memoranda on numerous aspects of the slavery problem, involving much of the world. A striking unit of its concern was Liberia, on the west

* J. C. McCoan, *Egypt as It Is* (1877), 25.

African coast, where slavery had not only been discovered, but where it involved some government officials directly in its mesh. (*See Reading No. 31*.) Liberia had been sponsored by Americans and by the Federal government as a haven for Negroes, and an outpost of their aspirations to independence and parity. That it should, however, inadvertently foster slavery gave one indication of the tenacious nature of the ancient tradition.

More important to slavery's physical vigor were social and international relations which prevented critics from attacking it forthrightly. Nations which sought the cooperation of overlords and leaders of lands where slavery was practiced usually found it convenient to ignore the fact in order to gain profit from oil concessions, other commercial relations, and shipping bases. Nor was it always possible to use superior force to overthrow a distasteful regime. Its leaders, though perhaps militarily weak, could appeal to another great power for "protection." It became inexpedient for even the most technologically advanced nation to force its interpretation of due social and human relations on nations which condoned servitude. Hence slavery could flourish with more or less harshness among the most modern appurtenances of civilization: motorcars, elevators, and air conditioners. As late as 1948, although the United Nations could prepare an International Bill of Human Rights (*see Reading No. 32*), it was couched in such general terms as to have no practical import.

But most important in the persistence of slavery, often with little effort at concealment, was the state of public opinion. It was generally partisan in a fashion which prevented reformers from congealing antislavery information and ideas effectively. The abolitionists of the nineteenth century had been able to find issues and eloquence which created an informed climate of opinion opposing slavery. The less technically advanced nations usually lacked a solid bloc of individualists and property holders to whom slavery represented serious competition and an intolerable psychological affront.

In the United States, as elsewhere, public opinion discriminated among foreign nations as it sympathized with one and was antipathetic to another. "Forced labor" was reprobated and rendered emotionally reprehensible when employed by one government, and interpreted sympathetically when utilized by another. Faith in one Middle Eastern or Far Eastern nation determined whether its local social traditions would or would not be scorned. Although Americans travelled more widely than ever, in greater democratic numbers, and not infrequently as "informal ambassadors" on government grants, they seemed rarely disturbed by social conditions in foreign lands on purely human grounds, at least enough to feel a need for action. Indeed, a penetrating documentary motion picture circulating in the United States, *Slavery in the World Today* (1964) offered candid exposures of slave practices. Though it was advertised in lurid terms intended to attract attention, and though it did draw interested audiences, it made no impression on any part of its audience, black or white, as a subject meriting consideration in depth, or of relating past to present.

The Future of Slavery. The tide of nationalism in underdeveloped countries which had once suffered a sense of enslavement to imperialist powers helped put the *concept* of slavery into bad repute. The *reality* of slavery appeared to continue to have good possibilities of survival and even growth in the future. It could even be condoned by elements which esteemed themselves as libertarian, but who paid insufficient attention to the human details which permitted a profound distinction between freedom and slavery. Assumptions that slavery was a thing of the past, or that it was a temporary aberration in the horrendous drama of a defunct Nazism, could only contribute to sustaining true slavery wherever it subsisted. A study of the contours of American slavery, and a comparison of them with comparable systems past and present, offered the best possibilities for improving understanding of slavery's place in human affairs.

Part II

READINGS

Andrew Jackson Seeks a Runaway[1]

Andrew Jackson (1767–1845) was one of the most hated and admired Americans of his time. A rough, combative lawyer, soldier, and politician, he won the regard of those who loved the country for the rewards it offered those who could fight and win, and the contempt of others who respected tradition and civilization, and who preferred diplomacy to war. Risen from poverty, Jackson ruled his Tennessee estate, the Hermitage, as he later ruled the United States: with a firm hand which brooked no contradiction. As a slave owner, he was normally kinder than some, and sharper than others when crossed, as in the following instance, culled from the Tennessee Gazette & Mero District Advertiser *(Nashville, Nov. 7, 1804).*

STOP THE RUNAWAY. FIFTY DOLLARS REWARD. Eloped from the subscriber, living near Nashville on the 25th. of June last, a Mulatto Man Slave, about thirty years old, five feet and an inch high, stout made and active, talks sensible, stoops in his walk, and has a remarkably large foot, broad across the root of the toes—will pass for a free man, as I am informed he has obtained by some means, certificates as such—took with him a drab great-coat, dark mixed body coat, a ruffled shirt, cotton home spun shirts and overalls. He will make for Detroit, through the states of Kentucky and Ohio, or the upper part of Louisiana. The above reward will be given any person that will take him and deliver him to me, or secure him in jail so that I can get him. If taken out of the state, the above reward, and all reasonable expenses paid—and ten dollars extra for every hundred lashes any person will give him to the amount of three hundred.

[1] Ulrich B. Phillips, ed., *Plantation and Frontier*, in *A Documentary History of American Industrial Society*, eds., John R. Commons, *et al.* (New York, 1958 ed.), II, 87–88.

Indian Slavers[2]

Northern states suppressed their Indian antagonists before the South was able to do so, and therefore, northern compassion for harassed southern Indian tribes, though often sincere, inevitably became political in temper. The case of the Cherokee was particularly acute because of the patent civilization they had attained, and the rude betrayal of treaties (particularly in Georgia) to which they were subjected. Indian reform was a minor cause during the pre-Civil War era, and was obscured by the attention paid Negroes by moral reformers. They were also repelled by the element of slavery in Indian affairs, as represented in the following selection. Goodell (1792–1878) was a businessman turned into a long-time moral reformer and abolitionist.

THE CHEROKEES

The "Constitution of the Cherokee Nation," formed by a Convention of Delegates from the several districts at New-Echota, July, 1827, contains the following:

"No person shall be eligible to a seat in General Council but a *free* Cherokee male citizen, who shall have attained to the age of twenty-five years. The descendants of Cherokee men by all *free* women, *except* the African race, whose parents may [have] been living together as man and wife, according to the customs and laws of this nation, shall be entitled to all the rights and privileges of this nation, as well as the posterity of Cherokee women by all *free* men. *No person who is of negro or mulatto parentage, either by the father or mother side, shall be eligible to hold any office of profit, honor, or trust in this Government.*" (Art. III., sect. 4.). . . .

Among the laws of the Cherokees we find one, Sept. 1839, entitled,

---

[2] William Goodell, *The American Slave Code in Theory and Practice: Its distinctive Features Shown by Its Statutes, Judicial Decisions, and Illustrative Facts* (New York, 1853), 245–247.

"An act to prevent amalgamation with *colored* persons," (meaning descendants of Africans,) just as if Cherokees were whites, and *not* "colored." Penalty, corporal punishment, not to exceed fifty stripes, and such intermarriages declared not to be lawful.

Another "Act," under date of Nov. 15, 1843, is "to *legalize* intermarriage with *white* men!". . . .

Another "Act," dated 22d October, 1841, is for "prohibiting the teaching of negroes to read and write." "*Be it enacted by the National Council,* That from and after the passage of this Act, it shall not be lawful for any person or persons whatever to teach any free negro or negroes *not of Cherokee blood,** or any slave belonging to any citizen or citizens of the nation, to read or write." The penalty annexed to a violation of this enactment is a fine of $100 to $500, at the discretion of the Court trying the offense.

"An Act in regard to free negroes," Dec. 2, 1842, directs "the sheriffs of the several districts" to notify free negroes to leave the limits of the nation by the 1st of Jan. 1843. If they refused to go, they were to be immediately expelled. "Sect. 4. Be it further enacted, That should any free negro or negroes be found guilty of aiding, abetting, or decoying any slave or slaves to leave his or their owner or employer, such free negro or negroes shall receive for each and every such offense one hundred lashes on the bare back, and be immediately removed from this nation."

From the preceding extracts of the Constitutions and Laws it would seem that "free negroes and mulattoes not of Cherokee blood" were not considered as "entitled to Cherokee privileges," or as constituting a part of "the Cherokee nation." And the teaching of them or the slaves to read or write, as has been shown, is expressly forbidden, under heavy penalties. So that the peculiar phraseology employed by the Bible Society is readily understood. Its object did not include the supply of such persons, and it was intended to guard against any such use of its funds! It is lamentable to see a nation so recently put in possession of the Bible, so forward to withhold it from others, even forbidding its use! But in this the Cherokees only imitate our own nation and our own Bible Societies, from whom they have received the Scriptures! They have only practised the religion they have received from us! We may see in this the fruit of sending to the heathen a gospel that tolerates slaveholding.

CHOCTAWS

The Constitution of the Choctaw Nation, approved October, 1838, embodies a "Declaration of Rights," the first article of which com-

* *"Not of Cherokee blood!"* It would be quite an improvement, should our Anglo-Saxon slave legislators imitate this by saying, *"not of English blood,"* in their statutes of this character.

mences with, "All *freemen,* when they form a social compact, are equal in rights," &c. It is not difficult to trace the parentage of this emendation of the Declaration of '76. It is revealed in the following:

"From and after the adoption of this Constitution, *no free negro, or any part negro, unconnected with Choctaw or Chickasaw blood,* shall be permitted to come and settle in the Choctaw nation." (Art. VIII., sect. 6.)

"No person who is *any part negro* shall ever be allowed to hold any office under this Government." (Art. VIII., sect. 14.)

"The General Council, when in session, shall have the power by law to naturalize and adopt as citizens of this nation, any Indian, or descendant of other Indian tribes, *except a negro or descendant of a negro.*" (Art. VIII., sect. 15.)

The following is an act approved 5th October, 1836: . . .

"*Be it further enacted, &c.,* That teaching slaves how to read, to write, or to sing in meeting-houses or schools, or in any open place, without the consent of the owner, or allowing them to sit at table with him, shall be sufficient ground to convict persons of favoring the principles and notions of Abolitionism.["]

It was provided also that no slave should "be in possession of any property or arms;" that if any slave infringed any Choctaw rights, he should "be driven out of company to behave himself;" and in case of his return and further intrusion, "he should receive ten lashes." But "any good honest slave shall be permitted to carry a gun, by having a pass from his master."

In 1838 it was enacted, "That from and after the passage of this law, if any person or persons, citizens of this nation, shall *publicly take up with a negro slave,** he or she so offending shall be liable to pay a fine of not less than ten dollars, nor exceeding twenty-five dollars, *and shall be separated;* and for a second offense of a similar nature the party shall receive not exceeding thirty-nine lashes nor less than five, on the bare back, *and shall be separated,* as the Court may determine."

"The Constitution and Laws of the Choctaw Nation," from which the preceding extracts are taken, bears the imprint of 1840, and the latest enactments it contains are dated Oct. 1839. But the "American Missionary," New-York, January, 1853, contains an account of some later enactments, taken from a Report made in 1848 by Mr. Treat, one of the Secretaries of the American Board of Commissioners for Foreign Missions. The following is an extract from this statement of the "American Missionary:" . . .

---

* "*Publicly take up with.*" The possibility of a *legal marriage* with a slave seems not to have been recognized. The union was only "a *taking up with,*" a phrase used among slaves.

" '*Be it enacted,* &c., That no negro slave can be emancipated in this Nation except by application or petition of the owner to the General Council; and *provided also,* that it shall be made to appear to the Council the owner or owners, at the time of application, shall have no debt or debts outstanding against him or her, either in or out of this Nation. Then, and in that case, the General Council shall have the power to pass an act for the owner to emancipate his or her slave, which negro, after being freed, shall leave this nation within thirty days after the passage of the Act. And in case said free negro or negroes shall return into this Nation afterwards, he, she, or they shall be subject to be taken by the light horsemen and exposed to public sale for the term of five years; and the funds arising from such sale shall be used as national funds.' "

The Slave Trader: His Life and Outlook[3]

John Newton (1725–1807), who became a distinguished author and minister, was a slave trader who turned upon his occupation. His Thoughts upon the African Slave Trade *(1788) was one of the notable indictments of the traffic, not only spelling out its tragic effects upon innumerable victims, but the manner in which it debased the moral sense of the slavers. He himself later marvelled at his own lack of scruples, during his activities on the Windward Coast, between the river Sierra Leone and Cape Palmas, from 1745 to 1754. Humiliated by his own career, he could only reason that what he had done, he had done in ignorance. No one had questioned his purposes, and he had treated his slaves "with as much humanity as a regard to my own safety would permit."*

Tuesday 22nd January [1750]. . . . No trade or traders to day to be heard of. In the evening came down the *Africa* from Junque and a ketch belonging to Cape Coast Castle called the *Pye,* master's name, Dun.

Wednesday 23rd January. . . . Yellow Will brought me off a boy slave, 3 foot 10 inches, which I was obliged to take or get nothing. . . .

Thursday 24th January. . . . No trade today. I only wait the return of William Freeman from Tabo caney to bring me my 2 slaves, and would proceed upwards immediately, but have heard nothing of him since he went away, which is now a week. The trade has now come to that pass that there is no getting a slave without sending the goods first on shoar, tho by that step we hazard losing their custom entirely, as may possibly be my case; and the farther to leeward, the dearer and more precarious.

Fryday 25th January. . . . Yellow Will brought me a woman slave, but being long breasted and ill made, refused her, and made him take her on

[3] John Newton, *The Journal of a Slave Trader,* ed. with intro. by Bernard Martin and Mark Spurrell (London, 1962), 32–33, 44, 47, 56.

shoar again, tho I am not certain I shall be able to get one in her room. He brought of a cask of palm oyl I gave him to fill, containing about 50 gallons, and 30 fowls. Loosed and aired the sails; got up the spare sails out of the hold, and overhalled them, found the rats have done them a good deal of damage we being quite over-run with them and can not get a cat upon any terms, and these we brought from England have been dead sometime. Finished the platforms in the women's room and stowed the sails there for the present. Sailed the *Pye* for Cape Coast. . . .

Thursday 31st January. . . . Detected Will Lapworth, one I had from on board the *Surprize,* of breaking the lock of the state room scuttle and stealing brandy; put him in irons. Loosed and aired the sails. No canoo's off to day; will try them to morrow and no longer. The *Pardoe* has been in sight all day working off and on, and in the evening perceived another snow coming up from the leeward.

Fryday 1st February. . . . Waited for a canoo with a good deal of impatience, but in vain for none came off. If the opportunity continues, propose to sail in the morning, and rather, because the *Bridget,* Grierson, went past upwards to day and told the *Africa's* boat who went off to her, that the trade is entirely ruined at Rio Sestors, and the *Adlington's* longboat lately cut off there, the mate and 1 more killed. The *Bridget* lost her yaul and mate upon little Sestors bar, in short not a vessel that I speak with or hear of but has met some misfortunes, which ought to silence my complaints, who have hither to been exempted from any but the customary lot of mortality. In the morning William Lapworth confessed the fact I confined him for. Turned him out of irons and gave him a smart dozen for a *caveto.* At 10 p.m. a longboat came down from to windward but did not speak her. . . .

Thursday 4th April [1751]. . . . At 4 a.m. the yaul filled astern and before we could get her alongside, overset. It was with a great deal of difficulty that we saved her, got the tackles on and hoisted her in upon deck, almost stove in pieces, but lost everything out of her, the rudder, mast and sail and 5 oars and a large graplin and rope. Repaired her as well as we could and turned her out again and sent her to the beach perceiving a smoke. Fitted her with the punt's oars and two broken ones belonging to the longboat. Going on shoar they picked up two more and the mast and sail. Mr Marshall came off in her, brought me the same boy from Mr Hall that I redeemed, he not being able to pay 2 slaves for him, tho he talked as if he was master of 20 when on board. Mr Clow answered my letter and says he will send me 5 slaves at 75 bars per head, which I allowed Mr Marshall to offer rather than lose his trouble: so I shall not think myself obliged to him at all if he sends, but beleive I shall sail before his boat comes. James Cumberbatch's shallop is at last come down with 4 or 5 slaves and I expect him on board to morrow.

Fryday 5th April. . . . Loosed and aired the sails, and likewise overhalled and aired the spare sails, found them much damaged by the rats, but know no help for it; stowed them away in the store room. In the morning sent Mr Hamilton in the shallop to return her to Mr Tucker, and in the afternoon sent the yaul to the beach to bring off our people, came back a sunset. I understand Cumberbatch is not yet come down, and Mr Osborne is afraid to bring the slaves on board without him lest I should detain all together. A guilty conscience haunts them all—they would willingly cheat me, but are afraid of being known to be what they are. . . .

Sunday 21st April. . . . Was obliged to wave the consideration of the day [the religious service for the crew] for the first and, I hope, the last time of the voyage, the season advancing fast and, I am afraid, sickness too; for we have almost every day one or more taken with a flux, of which a woman dyed to night (No. 79). I imputed it to the English provisions and have given them rice twice a day ever since I came here; a little time will show whether it agrees better with them than beans or pease. Started all our bread into the bean room, and the cooper prepared 5 of the 7 buts for water. The canoos from St Pauls brought off 24 casks of water and 5 load of wood. A canoo of Liverpool town that had 8 of our casks was stove last night going on shoar. They say they have saved the casks but I must send the yaul for them, they not having a canoo fit to bring them off. One [of] my traders brought about 300 lb rice. Captain Anyon discharged his trader, William Purcell of Liverpool; he came to me and I gave him some goods for rice for his former good behaviour and to encourage him to procure my 3 slaves that William Grey owed me, who dyed soon after I went to windward. He assures me I shall have them in a few days. . . .

Wednesday 12th June. . . . Got the slaves up this morn. Washed them all with fresh water. They complained so much of cold that was obliged to let them go down again when the rooms were cleaned. Buryed a man slave (No. 84) of a flux, which he has been strugling with near 7 weeks. . . .

Thursday 13th June. . . . This morning buryed a women slave (No. 47). Know not what to say she died of for she has not been properly alive since she first came on board.

Sunday 16th June. In the afternoon we were alarmed with a report that some of the men slaves had found means to poyson the water in the scuttle casks upon deck, but upon enquiry found they had only conveyed some of their country fetishes, as they call them, or talismans into one of them, which they had the credulity to suppose must inevitably kill all who drank of it. But if it please God thay make no worse attempts than to charm us to death, they will not much harm us, but it shews their intentions are not wanting. . . .

James Fenimore Cooper On Slavery in New York[4]

James Fenimore Cooper (1789–1851) was a striking compound of aristo-cratic principles and Jacksonian sympathies, which he interpreted to mean rule by the best. His "Leatherstocking" series of novels made him famous. He went on to quarrel with his public in fiction and essays in behalf of his élite upstate New York associates. These great landowners were reluctant to release any of their properties to their frustrated tenants, who defied statutes and constables in their fight for independence. Cooper's trilogy, the Little page Manuscripts, *included* Satanstoe (*1845*), The Chainbearer (*1846*), *and* The Redskins, or Indian and Injun (*1846*). These writings scorned the anti-rent rioters and praised a way of life which assumed slaves as well as tenants. Here Cooper describes a "Pinkster Frolic," a Negro slave celebra-tion in New York City.*

Jason was at first confounded with the noises, dances, music, and games that were going on. By this time nine-tenths of the blacks of the city, and of the whole country within thirty or forty miles, indeed, were collected in thousands in those fields, beating banjoes, singing African songs, drinking, and worst of all, laughing in a way that seemed to set their very hearts rattling within their ribs. Everything wore the aspect of good-humor, though it was good-humor in its broadest and coarsest forms. Every sort of common game was in requisition; while drinking was far from being neglected. Still, not a man was drunk. A drunken negro, indeed, is by no means a common thing. The features that distin-guish a Pinkster frolic from the usual scenes at fairs, and other merry-

[4] J. Fenimore Cooper, *Satanstoe* (New York, 1900), 61, 65–66.

makings, however, were of African origin. It is true, there are not now, nor were there then, many blacks among us of African birth; but the traditions and usages of their original country were so far preserved as to produce a marked difference between this festival and one of European origin. Among other things, some were making music by beating on skins drawn over the ends of hollow logs, while others were dancing to it in a manner to show that they felt infinite delight. This, in particular, was said to be a usage of their African progenitors.

Hundreds of whites were walking through the fields, amused spectators. Among these last were a great many children of the better class, who had come to look at the enjoyment of those who attended them, in their own ordinary amusements. Many a sable nurse did I see that day chaperoning her young master, or young mistress, or both together, through the various groups; demanding of all, and receiving from all, the respect that one of these classes was accustomed to pay to the other. . . .

New York never had slaves on the system of the southern planters, or in gangs of hundreds, to labor in the fields under overseers, and who lived apart in cabins of their own; but our system of slavery was strictly domestic, the negro almost invariably living under the same roof with the master, or, if his habitation was detached, as certainly sometimes happened, it was still near at hand, leaving both races as part of a common family. In the country, the negroes never toiled in the field, but it was as ordinary husbandmen; and, in the cases of those who labored on their own property, or as tenants of some extensive landlord, the black did his work at his master's side. Then all, or nearly all our household servants were, and still are, blacks, leaving that department of domestic economy almost exclusively in their hands, with the exception of those cases in which the white females busied themselves also in such occupations, united to the usual supervision of the mistresses. Among the Dutch, in particular, the treatment of the negro was of the kindest character, a trusty field-slave often having quite as much to say on the subject of the tillage and the crops, as the man who owned both the land he worked and himself. . . .

Lest the habits of this generation should pass away and be forgotten, of which I see some evidence, I will mention a usage that was quite common among the Dutch, and which has passed, in some measure, into the English that have formed connections with the children of Holland. Two of these intermarriages had so far brought the Littlepages within the pale, that the usage to which I allude was practised in my own case. The custom was this: When a child of the family reached the age of six or eight, a young slave of the same age and sex was given to him, or her, with some little formality, and from that moment the fortunes of the two were considered to be, within the limits of their respective pursuits and positions, as those of man and wife. It is true, divorces do occur, but it is only in cases of gross misconduct, and quite as often the misconduct is on the side of the master, as on that of the slave. A drunkard may get in debt, and be compelled to part with his blacks—this one among the rest; but this particular negro remains with him as long as anything remains. Slaves that seriously misbehave, are usually sent to the island, where the toil on the sugar plantations proves a very sufficient punishment.

Frederick Law Olmsted: An Antislavery Opinion in North Carolina[5]

Frederick Law Olmsted (1822–1903) prepared classic records of his travels through the slave country, published as A Journey in the Seaboard Slave States (*1856*), A Journey through Texas (*1857*), *and* A Journey in the Back Country (*1860*), *condensed as* The Cotton Kingdom (*1861*). *Olmsted went on to become one of the greatest of American landscape architects.*

July 16th [1854]—I stopped last night at the pleasantest house I have yet seen in the highlands; a framed house, painted white, with a log kitchen attached. The owner was a man of superior standing. I judged from the public documents and law books on his table, that he had either been in the Legislature of the State, or that he was a justice of the peace. There were also a good many other books and newspapers, chiefly of a religious character. He used, however, some singularly uncouth phrases common here. He had a store, and carried on farming and stock raising. After a conversation about his agriculture, I remarked that there were but few slaves in this part of the country. He wished that there were fewer. They were not profitable property here, I presumed. They were not, he said, except to raise for sale; but there were a good many people here who would not have them if they were profitable, and yet who were abundantly able to buy them. They were horrid things, he thought; he would not take one to keep it if it should be given to him. 'Twould be a great deal better for the country, he believed, if there was not a slave in it. He supposed it would not be right to take them away

[5] Frederick Law Olmsted, *The Cotton Kingdom,* ed. Arthur M. Schlesinger (New York, 1953), 398–400.

from those who had acquired property in them, without any remuneration, but he wished they could all be sent out of the country—sent to Liberia. That was what ought to be done with them. I said it was evident that where there were no slaves, other things being equal, there was greater prosperity than where slavery supplied the labour. He didn't care so much for that, he said; there was a greater objection to slavery than that, in his mind. He was afraid that there was many a man who had gone to the bad world, who wouldn't have gone there if he hadn't had any slaves. He had been down in the nigger counties a good deal, and he had seen how it worked on the white people. It made the rich people, who owned the niggers, passionate and proud, and ugly, and it made the poor people mean. "People that own niggers are always mad with them about something; half their time is spent in swearing and yelling at them."

"I see you have 'Uncle Tom's Cabin' here," said I; "have you read it?"

"Oh, yes."

"And what do you think of it?"

"Think of it? I think well of it."

"Do most of the people here in the mountains think as you do about slavery?"

"Well, there's some thinks one way and some another, but there's hardly any one here that don't think slavery's a curse to our country, or who wouldn't be glad to get rid of it."

I asked what the people about here thought of the Nebraska Bill. He couldn't say what the majority thought. Would people moving from here to Nebraska now, be likely to vote for the admission of slavery there? He thought not; "most people would much rather live in a Free State." He told me that he knew personally several persons who had gone to California, and taken slaves with them, who had not been able to bring them back. There were one or two cases where the negroes had been induced to return, and these instances had been made much of in the papers, as evidence that the slaves were contented.

"That's a great lie," he said; "they are not content, and nine-tenths of 'em would do 'most anything to be free. It's only now and then that slaves, who are treated unusual kind, and made a great deal of, will choose to remain in slavery if freedom is put in their way." He knew one man (giving his name) who tried to bring two slaves back from California, and had got started with them, when some white people suspecting it, went on board the ship and told him it was against the law to hold negroes as slaves in California, and his negroes shouldn't go back with him unless they were willing to. Then they went to the slaves and told them they need not return if they preferred to stay, and the slaves said they had wanted very much to go back to North Carolina, yet they would rather remain in California, if they could be free, and so they took them ashore. He had heard the slave owner himself relating this, and cursing the men who interfered. He had told him that they did no more than Christians were obliged to do.

Emancipation Proclamation: What It Did and Did Not Do[6]

Abraham Lincoln (1809–1865) was for many years revered by Negro and whites alike for his promulgation of the Emancipation Proclamation. Yet his views on the race question were plainly moderate, and it was the Thirteenth Amendment to the Constitution, and not the Proclamation, which ended slavery as a legal system in the United States. The Thirteenth Amendment, validated December 18, 1865, provided that "[n]either slavery nor involuntary servitude, except as a punishment for crime whereof the party shall have been duly convicted, shall exist within the United States, or any place subject to their jurisdiction." Close reading of the Proclamation, on the other hand, reveals that whether or not it wounded slavery as an institution, it did not expunge it. The Proclamation freed slaves wherever its people were in rebellion, and specifically ruled out from its provisions such parishes, counties, and cities in the South held by Federal troops, where slavery could have been immediately eradicated. The Proclamation asserted itself to be "a fit and necessary war measure," and no more. Lincoln's justification lay in his need to hold together for the Union states not yet ready to accept full emancipation. Their disaffection could have destroyed the Union effort, and riveted slavery within a triumphant Confederacy.

By The President of the United States of America:

A Proclamation.

Whereas on the 22nd day of September, A.D. 1862, a proclamation was

---

[6] Henry Steele Commager, ed., *Documents of American History* (New York, 1958), 420–421.

85

issued by the President of the United States, containing, among other things, the following, to wit:

"That on the 1st day of January, A.D. 1863, all persons held as slaves within any State or designated part of a State the people whereof shall then be in rebellion against the United States shall be then, thenceforward, and forever free; and the executive government of the United States, including the military and naval authority thereof, will recognize and maintain the freedom of such persons and will do no act or acts to repress such persons, or any of them, in any efforts they may make for their actual freedom.

"That the executive will on the 1st day of January aforesaid, by proclamation, designate the States and parts of States, if any, in which the people thereof, respectively, shall then be in rebellion against the United States; and the fact that any State or the people thereof shall on that day be in good faith represented in the Congress of the United States by members chosen thereto at elections wherein a majority of the qualified voters of such States shall have participated shall, in the absence of strong countervailing testimony, be deemed conclusive evidence that such State and the people thereof are not then in rebellion against the United States."

Now, therefore, I, Abraham Lincoln, President of the United States, by virtue of the power in me vested as Commander-in-Chief of the Army and Navy of the United States in time of actual armed rebellion against the authority and government of the United States, and as a fit and necessary war measure for suppressing said rebellion, do, on this 1st day of January, A.D. 1863, and in accordance with my purpose so to do, publicly proclaim for the full period of one hundred days from the first day above mentioned, order and designate as the States and parts of States wherein the people thereof, respectively, are this day in rebellion against the United States the following, to wit:

Arkansas, Texas, Louisiana (except the parishes of St. Bernard, Plaquemines, Jefferson, St. John, St. Charles, St. James, Ascension, Assumption, Terrebonne, Lafourche, St. Mary, St. Martin, and Orleans, including the city of New Orleans), Mississippi, Alabama, Florida, Georgia, South Carolina, North Carolina, and Virginia (except the forty-eight counties designated as West Virginia, and also the counties of Berkeley, Accomac, Northhampton, Elizabeth City, York, Princess Anne, and Norfolk, including the cities of Norfolk and Portsmouth), and which excepted parts are for the present left precisely as if this proclamation were not issued.

And by virtue of the power and for the purpose aforesaid, I do order and declare that all persons held as slaves within said designated States and parts of States are, and henceforward shall be, free; and that the Executive Government of the United States, including the military and naval authorities thereof, will recognize and maintain the freedom of said persons.

And I hereby enjoin upon the people so declared to be free to abstain from all violence, unless in necessary self-defense; and I recommend to them that, in all cases when allowed, they labor faithfully for reasonable wages.

And I further declare and make known that such persons of suitable condition will be received into the armed service of the United States to garrison forts, positions, stations, and other places, and to man vessels of all sorts in said service.

And upon this act, sincerely believed to be an act of justice, warranted by the Constitution upon military necessity, I invoke the considerate judgment of mankind and the gracious favor of Almighty God.

"Codes" and the Negro:
Their Purpose and Variety[7]

"Slave Codes" and "Black Codes" were expressions often used interchangeably, though one attempted to define the status of slaves, the other of free Negroes. Black *Codes emphasized color and white supremacy, as in the 1670 Virginia enactment preventing free Negroes and Indians from owning white servants. Later, enslavement became more important than color, since not a few Negroes were lighter in complexion than their masters and mistresses. Thus,* Slave *Codes dominated their lives and opportunities.* Black *Codes more properly described ordinances, especially in the nominally free states along the border of the Mason-Dixon Line and the Ohio River. (See also Reading 8.) Both codes were bitterly denounced by abolitionists during the crusade against slavery, as in the following selection.*

An ox cannot buy himself of his owner, nor transfer himself to the ownership of another. Here again, "to all intents, constructions, and purposes whatsoever," the slave is on a level with other working chattels! This must be his predicament in the very nature of the case, if the principle of *chattelhood* is to be consistently maintained.

"Slaves cannot redeem themselves, nor obtain a change of masters, though cruel treatment may have rendered such a change necessary for their personal safety."

It is of American slavery in the nineteenth century of the Christian era, and among a people boasting their pure religion and their free institutions, that this is affirmed. Among ancient heathen nations were found laws providing that slaves abused by their masters might apply to the magistrates, who would order them to be sold to a new master.

[7] Goodell, *op. cit.*, 245–247.

In Mississippi, as before noticed, the Constitution has *empowered* the Legislature to enact such a law, but the Legislature have not seen fit to exercise the power.

In Louisiana, the new Civil Code contains a regulation looking apparently in that direction, but difficult, if not impossible, to be made effective. It is as follows:

"No master shall be compelled to sell his slave, but in one of two cases, to wit: the first, when, being only co-proprietor of the slave, his co-proprietor demands the sale, in order to make a partition of the property; *second,* when the master shall be CONVICTED of cruel treatment of his slave, *and the Judge shall deem it proper* to pronounce, besides the penalty established for such cases, that the slave shall be sold at public auction, in order to place him out of the reach of the power which his master has abused." (Art. 192.)

It is to be noticed here, that the Judge is only *empowered,* not *directed,* to make such a decree. He *may* apply merely the *other* penalties alluded to. . . . The master must be CONVICTED of cruelty by "WHITE" testimony, by a Court and jury of slaveholders, and amid legal rules and usages that expressly authorize chastisement with rigor, provided it be not *"unusual,"* nor "so as to maim or mutilate," or endanger life. (Civil Code of Louisiana.)

It is not known that this law of Louisiana has ever been enforced, and no other slave State in the Union, so far as we know, has any similar provision, though they are careful to provide, in this particular, for the security of *indented apprentices.* Without a *change of masters,* it is evident that no *other* laws against cruelty would be of any value. To punish an owner or overseer for abusing a slave, (even if it ever were done,) and then send the slave back again to be under the power of the same tyrant, (enraged, as he would be, at his punishment,) would only be to secure fresh injuries in secret.

The Northern Response to Freedmen[8]

John Randolph of Roanoke, Virginia (1773–1833) was so ardent a Jeffersonian that he turned on Jefferson himself when he became convinced that, as President, his leader had subverted their common principles. Randolph, an emotional thinker, mixed libertarian with states-rights ideas. He defended slavery, but provided for his slaves. "John Randolph's Negroes" were often noted in the course of the anti-slavery debate. The following is a news item from the New Orleans Commercial Times, *July 10, 1846.*

MANUMITTED SLAVES. Three hundred and eighty-five manumitted slaves, freed by the will of the late John Randolph, of Roanoke, passed through Cincinnati, on the 1st. instance, on their way to Mercer County, Ohio, where a large tract of land is provided for their future homes. The *Times,* of that city, understands that the law of that State, known as the Black Law, requiring every colored person coming into the country to give security not to become a public charge, will be rigidly put in force, in this instance. Judging from the proceedings of a late public meeting in Mercer County, we imagine this to be true.

[8] Phillips, *op. cit.,* II, 143.

Conditions Affecting Slavery:

Illinois and the West Indies[9]

British emancipation in the West Indies during the 1830's became to American abolitionists an exciting challenge to emulation. Less well realized is the fact that American conditions fostering freedom and opportunity impressed Britishers dissatisfied with slavery aspects of their own colonial structure. Illinois was received into the Union as a state in 1818 without slavery, despite the presence of a strong proslavery party, which then proceeded to agitate for changes in the state constitution to reverse that stipulation. An American pamphlet arguing against reversal was reprinted in England, and recommended for consideration with respect to the West Indies as well.

In the State of Illinois the price of labour is far above what may be regarded as its natural standard; for the wages of one day will support the labourer for several days. The causes of this are, the plenty and cheapness of land and provision, and the scarcity of labourers. A man readily earns enough money to purchase a small farm, and naturally prefers the condition of a farmer to that of a day labourer. From this cause it arises that more land than can be tilled by the farmer and his children is an incumbrance, or at least useless to him. The owner of large tracts may find it difficult to procure free labourers; and to him, in this state of affairs, the labour of Slaves may possibly be cheaper than that of Free Men. But the prosperity of this individual does not necessarily increase that of the State. The real value of labour is the same in this as in all other cases;

[9] *The Injurious Effects of Slave Labour: An Impartial Appeal to the Reason, Justice, and Patriotism of the People of Illinois* . . . (London, 1824), 8–9.

and its high price, in the present instance, only enables the labourer the sooner to commence proprietor, and enjoy the whole profit of his industry himself; thus distributing, as it were, into a thousand channels, that wealth which, in the case of the large Slave-holder, goes to swell a single stream. In the early stage of a settlement, the employment of Slaves enables rich individuals to bring an excess of agricultural products into the market for exportation, and thus create enormous fortunes. This, however, is not always a real indication of prosperity: it is often but drawing for present use upon the future resources of the country; and if the introduction of Slaves be a virtual exclusion of Free Labourers, as it has universally been found to be, it is the infliction of an incurable wound upon the future growth of the nation.

One of the most remarkable experiments that has yet been made upon the value of Free and Slave labour, was tried by the Hon. Joshua Steele, of Barbadoes. He was owner of an estate of nearly three hundred Slaves, and tried with great success the plan of paying them for task-work. Being put (without a premium) to work in the common manner, eighteen of the same Negroes did not do as much in a given time as six had performed a few days before with a small reward. His experiments ended in his giving regular wages, which the industry he had excited among his whole gang enabled him to pay. An alteration was made in the mode of governing the Slaves: the whips were taken from the overseers, all arbitrary punishments were abolished, and all offenses were tried, and sentence passed, by a Negro Court. His people became contented; and in little better than four years the annual net clearance of his estate was more than tripled. Who does not perceive that he had virtually changed his Slaves into Free Men, by awakening in them the love of gain, the feelings of emulation, and the sense of self-dependence?

A Slave Defends Slavery[10]

Solomon Northup averred that while living in Saratoga Springs, N.Y., in the 1830's, he often conversed with slaves brought north by their masters, and that, while always well dressed and provided for, the slaves confided that "they cherished a secret desire for liberty." How real the desire was is a matter of judgment, as was the loyalty and regard which some slaves accorded their masters. A pamphlet by a Georgia slave, a bootmaker, said to have been written over a number of years, offered a consistent argument in opposition to abolitionism. It held that Negroes were not and could not actually be free anywhere in the nation, that happiness resided in recognizing this fact, and that agitation was no more than driving slaveholders to tighten the bonds of their slave property. The pamphlet was said to have been published for the slave's "benefit and profit."

You must recollect, fanatical sirs, that the Slave children and their young masters and mistresses, are all raised up together. They suck together, play together, go a hunting together, go a fishing together, go in washing together, and, in a great many instances, eat together in the cotton-patch, sing, jump, wrestle, box, fight boy fights, and dance, together; and every other kind of amusement that is calculated to bolt their hearts together when grown up. You had better mind how you come here, and jump aboard of our masters; for I tell you, though we sometimes fight among ourselves, if another man jumps on either, we both pitch into him. You must recollect, that we are not oppressed here like your nominally free there. We can go into our masters' houses and get plenty of good things to eat; and we can shake hands with the big-bugs of the country, and walk side-by-side with Congress members on the side-

[10] Harrison Berry, *Slavery and Abolitionism, as Viewed by a Georgia Slave* (Atlanta, Ga., 1861), 26, 34.

93

walks, and stand and converse with gentlemen of the highest rank, for hours at a time. So, in short, we can do anything, with the exceptions of those privileges wrested from us in consequence of your diabolical, infernal, Black Republican, Abolition, fanatical agitation. . . .

. . . Who are you, who call yourselves my friends?—who cause me to be ten times worse oppressed, by your pretended friendship? Who are you, who say that all men, by the teaching of the Higher Law, should be free? when, at the same time, that very Law contradicts it, and shows, conclusively, that from the earliest period to the present day, one man was commanded to serve the other. Who are you, who deny that persons have been born Slaves prior to the enslavement of the Africans in America? when St. Paul said, nearly two thousand years ago, when speaking to a multitude of feud makers, such as you are, that he was *free-born;* showing, most conclusively, that all men *were not so born* in his day. Who are you, who say that the oppression of the Slaves of the South, is the prime cause of your sympathy? when you know that your pretended sympathy oppresses the Slave ten-fold more. Who are you, who hate your brother Southerner, and accuse him of bringing reproach and disgrace upon the Republic? when he is actually doing more for the protection of the country than you are, for, whereas, you employ men to work in your manufactories until you are overwhelmed with wealth, made on the labor of the poor men working for such small wages, barely sufficient to keep them comfortable while in the bloom of youth. What becomes of them when bowed down with old age, without a penny in their pockets? Are they not thrown on the public? . . .

John J. Audubon Encounters a Runaway[11]

Runaway slaves were of various types and conditions. Some were individuals who, fearing punishment for an alleged fault, hid in a brake or a swamp for a day or a fortnight before venturing back to the plantation. Others were more resolute in seeking freedom, or had the wit and education enabling them to undertake a long drive to freedom. During the abolitionist crusade, writers publicized the experiences of runaways the caliber of Harriet Tubman and Frederick Douglass, and helped make their potential known to northerners. Early in the 1820's, John J. Audubon (1780?–1851), one of the greatest of American naturalists, while hunting the specimens which made him famous, crossed the path of a runaway in a Louisiana bayou. He was typical of many runaways who lacked opportunities for elaborate strategies. Audubon's view of his circumstances may be contrasted to that with which Harriet Beecher Stowe later persuaded the North.

[Audubon was brought, by devious bayou paths, to a rude shelter wherein were the runaway's wife and three children. "Master," the slave said, "my wife, though black, is as beautiful to me as the President's wife is to him; she is my queen, and I look on our young ones as so many princes."]

Supper over, the fire was completely extinguished, and a small lighted pine-knot placed in a hollowed calabash. Seeing that both the husband and wife were desirous of communicating something to me, I at once and fearlessly desired them to unburden their minds; when the Runaway told me a tale of which the following is the substance.

About eighteen months before, a planter residing not very far off, having met with some losses, was obliged to expose his slaves at a public

[11] John James Audubon, *Delineations of American Scenery and Character*, intro. Francis Hobart Herrick (New York, 1926), 121–123.

sale. The value of his negroes was well known, and on the appointed day, the auctioneer laid them out in small lots, or offered them singly, in the manner which he judged most advantageous to their owner. The Runaway, who was well known as being the most valuable next to his wife, was put up by himself for sale, and brought an immoderate price. For his wife, who came next, and alone, eight hundred dollars were bidden and paid down. Then the children were exposed, and, on account of their breed, brought high prices. The rest of the slaves went off at rates corresponding to their qualifications.

The Runaway chanced to be purchased by the overseer of the plantation; the wife was bought by an individual residing about a hundred miles off, and the children went to different places along the river. The heart of the husband and father failed him under this dire calamity. For awhile he pined in deep sorrow under his new master; but having marked down in his memory the names of the different persons who had purchased each dear portion of his family, he feigned illness, if indeed he whose affections had been so grievously blasted could be said to feign it, refrained from food for several days, and was little regarded by the overseer, who felt himself disappointed in what he had considered a bargain.

On a stormy night, when the elements raged with all the fury of a hurricane, the poor Negro made his escape, and, being well acquainted with all the neighboring swamps, at once made directly for the cane brake, in the centre of which I found his camp. A few nights afterwards he gained the abode of his wife, and the very next after their meeting he led her away. The children one after another he succeeded in stealing, until at last the whole objects of his love were under his care.

To provide for five individuals was no easy task in those wilds, which, after the first notice was given of the wonderful disappearance of this extraordinary family, were daily ransacked by armed planters. Necessity, it is said, will bring the wolf from the forest. The Runaway seems to have well understood the maxim, for under night he approached his first master's plantation, where he had ever been treated with the greatest kindness. The house servants knew him too well not to aid him to the best of their power, and at the approach of each morning he returned to his camp with an ample supply of provisions. One day, while in search of wild fruits, he found a bear dead before the muzzle of a gun that had been set for the purpose. Both articles he carried to his home. His friends at the plantation managed to supply him with some ammunition, and in damp and cloudy days he first ventured to hunt around his camp. Possessed of courage and activity, he gradually became more careless, and rambled farther in search of game. It was on one of his excursions that I met him, and he assured me that the noise which I made in passing the *bayou* had caused him to lose the chance of killing a fine deer, although, said he, "my old musket misses fire sadly too often."

The runaways, after disclosing their secret to me, both rose from their seat, with eyes full of tears. "Good master, for God's sake, do something for us and our children," they sobbed forth with one accord. Their little ones lay sound asleep in the fearlessness of their innocence. Who could have heard such a tale without emotion? I promised them my most cordial assistance. They both sat up that night to watch my repose, and I slept close to their urchins, as if on a bed of the softest down.

Day broke so fair, so pure, and so gladdening, that I told them such heavenly appearances were ominous of good, and that I scarcely doubted of obtaining their full pardon. I desired them to take their children with them, and promised to accompany them to the plantation of their first master. They gladly obeyed. My Ibises were hung around their camp, and, as a memento of my having been there, I notched several trees, after which I bade adieu, perhaps for the last time, to that cane brake. We soon reached the plantation, the owner of which, with whom I was well acquainted, received me with all the generous kindness of a Louisiana planter. Ere an hour had elapsed, the Runaway and his family were looked upon as his own. He afterwards repurchased them from their owners, and treated them with his former kindness; so that they were rendered as happy as slaves generally are in that country, and continued to cherish that attachment to each other which had led to their adventures. Since this event happened, it has, I have been informed, become illegal to separate slave families without their consent.

John C. Calhoun Responds to Abolitionists[12]

John C. Calhoun (1782–1850) emerged as the most deeply committed southern spokesman working within the context of national expectations. His resolutions offered in the United States Senate, December 27, 1837, were intended to affirm the right of the slave states to be secure in their property, to receive defense from the assaults of abolitionists, and to expand their territorial holdings into Texas and elsewhere. The following day he elaborated on the resolutions, taking special note of the argument that the abolitionists were not disunionists, that they aimed only at freeing a handful of slaves in the District of Columbia and the Territories, and that they constituted a weak, frail group, including "a large portion of females."

But [Calhoun] had received a letter that very morning from one of the fraternity, of high standing and authority, which gave a very different account of the small corps of humble beggars. He says that they count 1,500 societies, averaging 100 individuals each, and are growing at the rate of one society a day. Here then, we have 150,000 persons regularly organized, with a copious revenue, and an extensive and powerful press (a large portion of whom are the Senator's constituents), who are waging regular war on the institutions of the Southern and Western States—institutions that involve not less than $900,000,000 of property, and the prosperity and safety of an entire section of this Union, in violation of the most solemnly plighted faith, and subversion of the fundamental principles of the constitution; and yet the Senator can see neither harm nor danger in all this. When we see one of his enlightened understanding, and usually correct sentiments, thus thinking and feeling, what must be the tone of those with whom he is daily associated, which could so blind his understanding, and blunt his moral perception?

[12] *The Works of John C. Calhoun* (New York, 1853), III, 160–163.

He next tells us that the abolitionists can do no harm—that their publications cannot circulate in the slaveholding States, and can do no mischief in the non-slaveholding States—that the evil exists here, where too much excitement exists—and that if we would keep perfectly cool and patient, and hear ourselves and constituents called robbers and murderers, and our rights, and property, and lives attacked, without moving hand or tongue, all would be well. Accustomed as he has been, to respect the Senator for his sober and correct judgment and feelings on most subjects, he could not but be surprised at the language which he has held on the present occasion. Is his judgment so perverted that he can see no danger to the constitution and the Union, for which he professes—and, he doubted not, sincerely—to have so much regard, in the thousands of publications and lectures which are daily issued and delivered, holding up, in the blackest colors, the character and the institutions of nearly one-half of the Union; exciting towards them the deepest feelings of abhorrence, to be returned, on their part, with a detestation not less deep? Is the universal spread of this deep, mutual abhorrence, compatible with the existence of the Union? If not, is it not time to arrest it, and, of course, to deliberate on the means of doing it? Are the Senator's reason and feelings so far warped, either that he cannot apprehend the plainest consequences, or apprehending, is indifferent to them? . . .

The Senator asks, Why mingle abolition with political matters? Why with the Texas question? He knew not how to reconcile such questions with the respect which he has entertained for the Senator's intelligence and fairness. Does not the Senator know that we have received hundreds of petitions, and that they continued daily to pour in on us in one incessant stream, praying that Texas may not be admitted, on the ground that it would extend the limits of the slaveholding portion of the Union? Does he not know that a sovereign State of the Union has come here with its resolutions objecting to the annexation on the same ground? Does he not know, that the entire movement on abolition, with the object proposed to be effected, and the means by which it is to be done, involves political and constitutional questions and considerations of the highest possible magnitude, vital to the peace and safety of all? Knowing all this, with what propriety could he ask me the question he did? Does he wish to shift the burden, by making those who repel, and not those who assail, responsible? Does he wish to transfer the odium from those who make war on our rights and property, to us, who defend them—and this, too, in the face of the most notorious facts?

Brief as has been his notice of the Senator's apology for the abolitionists (for such he must consider his speech), it is much longer than he would have made it, had it not been for the respect which he has had for his talents and character. He cannot consider the course he has pursued in his speech as indicative of his actual feelings and fairness, and is compelled to regard it as indicative of the distempered state of the public sentiment of those he represented. Thus viewed, it affords an important lesson to those he represented. Throughout, not a censure of the abolitionists is whispered. All is excuse, defence, apology. It is we, and not they who are the agitators; it is we, not they, who are the disturbers of the peace and quiet of the country; it is we, not they, who are the assailants; it is we, not they, who harbor ambitious and improper designs; and finally, it is we, not they, who meditate disunion. It is no crime to attack us, but a heinous offence in us to defend ourselves.

The Free Negro: His Enslavement[13]

The oppressed circumstances of free Negroes in the South could be perceived in the numerous threats to his actual freedom—because he had allegedly aided runaways, because he had incurred fines he could not pay, because he had left a slave state and illegally returned, and numerous other reasons including that he was unable to prove he was a free man. The Slave Codes spelled out such restrictions in great detail, bitterly so in the accounts given of them in abolitionist versions. Free Negroes in the North also lived within the shadow of enslavement, thanks to the bold, practiced competence of slave-catchers, and the uncertain execution of fugitive slave laws. Thus, a New York statute of 1840 theoretically protected the rights of its free citizens, yet a narrative published in 1853 disturbed a sensitized North with its account of a free Negro of Saratoga Springs, New York, a man of education and enterprise, who had been kidnapped in Washington, D.C. in 1841, and sold at auction for slavery on a Louisiana cotton plantation. Solomon Northup (1808– ?) was rescued in 1853 by a remarkable series of events which enabled his wife to learn of his whereabouts and plight and to win the aid of the governor of New York to effect his release. Northup's literacy and keen sense of the contrast between his birthright freedoms and the conditions of slavery made his one of the most effective of memoirs.

We were met at the door of Goodin's yard by that gentleman himself —a short, fat man, with a round, plump face, black hair and whiskers, and a complexion almost as dark as some of his own negroes. He had a hard, stern look, and was perhaps about fifty years of age. Burch and he met with great cordiality. They were evidently old friends. Shaking each other warmly by the hand, Burch remarked he had brought some com-

[13] Solomon Northup, *Twelve Years a Slave* . . . (New York, 1857), 59, 60–61, 240–241, 274.

pany, inquired at what time the brig would leave, and was answered that it would probably leave the next day at such an hour. Goodin then turned to me, took hold of my arm, turned me partly round, looked at me sharply with the air of one who considered himself a good judge of property, and as if estimating in his own mind about how much I was worth.

"Well, boy, where did you come from?"

Forgetting myself, for a moment, I answered, "From New-York."

"New-York! H—l! what have you been doing up there?" was his astonished interrogatory.

Observing Burch at this moment looking at me with an angry expression that conveyed a meaning it was not difficult to understand, I immediately said, "O, I have only been up that way a piece," in a manner intended to imply that although I might have been as far as New-York, yet I wished it distinctly understood that I did not belong to that free State, nor to any other. . . .

Burch and Goodin, after separating from us, walked up the steps at the back part of the main building, and sat down upon the door sill. They entered into conversation, but the subject of it I could not hear. Presently Burch came down into the yard, unfettered me, and led me into one of the small houses.

"You told that man you came from New-York," said he.

I replied, "I told him I had been up as far as New-York, to be sure, but did not tell him I belonged there, nor that I was a freeman. I meant no harm at all, Master Burch. I would not have said it had I thought."

He looked at me a moment as if he was ready to devour me, then turning round went out. In a few minutes he returned. "If ever I hear you say a word about New-York, or about your freedom, I will be the death of you—I will kill you; you may rely on that," he ejaculated fiercely.

I doubt not he understood then better than I did, the danger and the penalty of selling a free man into slavery. He felt the necessity of closing my mouth against the crime he knew he was committing. Of course, my life would not have weighed a feather, in any emergency requiring such a sacrifice. Undoubtedly, he meant precisely what he said. . . .

There was not a day throughout the ten years I belonged to Epps that I did not consult with myself upon the prospect of escape. I laid many plans, which at the time I considered excellent ones, but one after the other they were all abandoned. No man who has never been placed in such a situation, can comprehend the thousand obstacles thrown in the way of the flying slave. Every white man's hand is raised against him— the patrollers are watching for him—the hounds are ready to follow on his track, and the nature of the country is such as renders it impossible to pass through it with any safety. I thought, however, that the time might come, perhaps, when I should be running through the swamps again. I concluded, in that case, to be prepared for Epps' dogs, should they pursue me. He possessed several, one of which was a notorious slave-hunter, and the most fierce and savage of his breed. While out hunting the coon or the opossum, I never allowed an opportunity to escape, when alone, of whipping them severely. In this manner I succeeded at length in subduing them completely. They feared me, obeying my voice at once when others had no control over them whatever. Had they followed and overtaken me, I doubt not they would have shrank from attacking me.

Notwithstanding the certainty of being captured, the woods and swamps are, nevertheless, continually filled with runaways. Many of them, when sick, or so worn out as to be unable to perform their tasks, escape into the swamps, willing to suffer the punishment inflicted for such offences, in order to obtain a day or two of rest. . . .

I am often asked, with an air of incredulity, how I succeeded so many years in keeping from my daily and constant companions the knowledge of my true name and history. The terrible lesson Burch taught me, impressed indelibly upon my mind the danger and uselessness of asserting I was a freeman. There was no possibility of any slave being able to assist me, while, on the other hand, there *was* a possibility of his exposing me. When it is recollected the whole current of my thoughts, for twelve years, turned to the contemplation of escape, it will not be wondered at, that I was always cautious and on my guard. It would have been an act of folly to have proclaimed my *right* to freedom; it would only have subjected me to severer scrutiny—probably have consigned me to some more distant and inaccessible region than even Bayou Bœuf. Edwin Epps was a person utterly regardless of a black man's rights or wrongs—utterly destitute of any natural sense of justice, as I well knew. It was important, therefore, not only as regarded my hope of deliverance, but also as regarded the few personal privileges I was permitted to enjoy, to keep from him the history of my life.

Colonization and the Free Negro[14]

Colonization acquired an infamous reputation as a result of the assaults of abolitionists. However, it attracted earnest and distinguished individuals, and had patently promising aspects. Thus, Benjamin Lundy (1789–1839), a pioneer abolitionist, made great efforts to colonize Negroes in Canada, in Texas, and in Haiti. His goal was to provide opportunities for self-improvement for free Negroes, to encourage slaveholders to manumit slaves for whose safety they might fear in a slavery-supporting nation, and to provide dramatic proof of the ability of Negroes to administer their own affairs and to improve their holdings of land and resources. Some of these reasons inspired founders of the American Colonization Society in 1816, who attracted Federal and philanthropic support North and South. However, impatient abolitionists came to believe that the main goal of colonization was not to stir up a wave of manumissions of slaves, but to rid the country of free Negroes. Garrison's Thoughts on African Colonization . . . *(1832) was a wounding blow to the Society's prestige. William Jay's* Inquiry into the Character and Tendency of the American Colonization and American Anti-Slavery Societies *(1835) was an all but mortal blow.*

Q.4. They have to eat *roots* there. They cannot get any bacon and cabbage there, nor any thing like what we live on here.

A.4. Is there anything in the climate or soil of Liberia that should make *roots* more unwholesome or unpalatable as an article of food there than they are in this country? It is a fact that they eat *roots* there, and so they do here, and in the form of sweet potatoes, Irish potatoes, turnips, &c. They are here generally much admired, and we see no good reason why the same thing should not be true of them in Liberia.

There is no danger of starvation in Liberia. There is no difficulty in

[14] *Common Objections to Going to Liberia Answered* (n.p., n.d.), 2–4.

getting plenty to eat, of good wholesome food. It is true that some articles of diet eaten here cannot be gotten there without much inconven-
ience. But it is also true that there are many vegetables and fruits there,
which are not found here; and that nature has furnished an abundant
supply of the kind of food best calculated to promote the health and
comfort of people living on that soil, and in that climate. . . .

Q.1. Why do the whites wish to get clear of us, and send us away to
that land?

A.1. It is not true that the friends of colonization are actuated by no
higher motive than "to get clear of the colored people." They do not propose to *send* them to Liberia contrary to their own wishes. Their will is
always consulted in the matter. We have no power to *send* them. They
can stay here as long as they wish. But our opinion is that their stay in
this country will ever be attended with such depressing influences as to
render it anything but desirable. While, on the contrary, their departure
to Liberia will bring them into an entirely new set of circumstances,
where a vast field of advancement will be opened to them, and the most
powerful motives be brought to bear upon them to lift them up in the
scale of being. In this country we see no prospect of their ever rising
above their present level. There no power can prevent them from rising.

Another consideration on this point. If we wish to *get clear* of them,
and this only, we certainly are laboring with but very little prospect of
obtaining our *wish.* The number transported to Liberia bears so little
comparison to their natural increase, that to continue the progress with
no other motive than merely to *get clear* of them, would be the blankest
business in the wide world. This, therefore, cannot be the reason why we
give and labor to support colonization, and urge its claims and benefits
upon them, from time to time, with all the ardor of our minds.

Q.2. If we must live by ourselves, why do you not give us some place
in the United States, where there is room enough?

A.2. Will they please to designate what particular place in the United
States they would like to have assigned to them? Where is there a spot
not wanted by the white man? How rapidly is our population spreading
over the whole country? What has been the fate of the poor Indian?
Where is his resting place? Where his home, not ever to be disturbed by
the march of civilization? Could the colored people hope for a better
destiny than has been his?

Will they go west of the Rocky Mountains? Ask them. And if they
were there and comfortably fixed, what assurance have they, that their
descendants will be allowed quietly to remain there? . . .

Colonization and the Slave[15]

Free Negroes, particularly in the North, resisted colonization, as it in-tended to drive them from their native homes, but it was a tragic illusion for ambitious slaves to whom it seemed to promise freedom, and whose masters were unaffected by its lure. The slave who wrote the following and other let-ters to the American Colonization Society was serving his own people as a minister. His hope and enthusiasm was to no avail; no money materialized to purchase his bondage.

RICHMOND VA June 21st 1847.

Dear Respected Brother I write to inform you—that I am what is here term a private African Slave Minister belonging to Mr. John Cosby of this city and My determination if possible is to go to Liberia let it cost what it may. This resolution I came to for more than 9 months ago and I have made Many Applications to our Methodist Ministers here to send me as a missionary to some vacant field in Africa and they Spurn me away Saying that they could do nothing for me in these respects if I were not a free Man. So I continue asking them up to the 30th of last May at which time they agreed to send Me as a Mission but they did not agree to raise the funds to buy me, if it should be needful. So now I intend to ask My Master to let me go on free cost to said Liberia and should he deny me then will I beg him to sell me for that purpose and should I do this I wish to have the Good Brothers of Colonization Society to be here to buy me immediately for the purpose mensioned above Dear Sire I wish you to know that the only object I have in view is my God & the Glory of his Son and in these Southern States We African Sons in the

[15] Carter G. Woodson, ed., *The Mind of the Negro as Reflected in Letters Written during the Crisis, 1800–1860* (Washington, D.C., 1926), 15–16.

church of God are Cut off for our part So that we can not become wise unto Salvation our selves and can not be the instrument in the hand of God in turning Many to Righteousness and the deprivation of church Rights & priviledges here has made me willing and ready to give up this part of the world & any other object for the Sake of Christ and the Glory of his people in that continant   Dear Sire a potion of our Methodist Ministers of the South has So repeatedly defeated me in my attempt that I could not avoid writing to you hoping and praying that God may help you to undertake My case and advocate My cause if needful among the Northern Ministers and people   Dear Sire Mr. John Cosby bought me about 17 years ago and Should he purpose to sell me to myself or to the Society he will not charge more than half as much as he then payed for me which would be about $150 for he only give $300 for me 17 years ago   Dear Sire you here See the object which I have in view and if it is in your power to come to Richmond now or in a short time you will please do So, if not, you will please send Some one to this city to see Me and My Master and if this can not be done I pray you Dear kind friend to write to me and teach Me what to do or if not Write to Rev. Mr. Edwards of Centenary church and teach him the facts that is here written that he may call for me and hear my determination and rewrite to you on My behalf & do whatever is proper to be done in this matter. My name is Bureell W. Mann now belonging to Mr. John Cosby and now working at the tobacco factory of Mr. Daid M. Branch on the Bassin and attached to the Methodist church, on union hill, in Richmond, under the charge of Rev. Joseph Carson. My little Talent & usefulness can be obtained by writing but I rather you would come your self or Send Some one if possible   I and am a poor christian here and wishing to get Good and do all the Good I can while I live on the earth but there is a very Small chants of doing Much Good in these Southern States——I ever remain your humble Servant, in Christ Jesus, Bureel W. Mann

The Folklore of Rebellion:

The Appeal of Nat Turner[16]

Rumors, fears, and events produced a canon of writings about slave upris-
ings which were emotionally received by proslavery spokesmen who wished to
stifle all protestants, and by antislavery partisans who eagerly sought all evi-
dence that Negroes were unnaturally confined as slaves. The Nat Turner in-
cident of 1831 partly attained fame because of the drama of an inspired
leader of blacks, their bloody assault on whites in Southampton County, Vir-
ginia, and the ruthless suppression of the insurrectionists in retaliation. But
Nat Turner survived mainly because of his alleged "confession" to one
Thomas R. Gray: a relatively brief, but evocative statement of purpose and
actions. This "confession" developed a lore of its own which has only today
been systematically examined and implemented by fresh material.

As I was praying one day at my plough, the spirit spoke to me, saying
"Seek ye the kingdom of Heaven and all things shall be added unto you.
QUESTION—What do you mean by the Spirit. ANS. The Spirit that
spoke to the prophets in former days. . . . Now finding I had arrived to
man's estate, and was a slave, and these revelations being made known
to me, I began to direct my attention to this great object, to fulfil the purpose for which, by this time, I felt assured I was intended. Knowing the
influence I had obtained over the minds of my fellow servants, (not by
the means of conjuring and such like tricks—for to them I always spoke
of such things with contempt) but by the communion of the Spirit whose
revelations I often communicated to them, and they believed and said
my wisdom came from God. I now began to prepare them for my pur-

[16] Henry Irving Tragle, *The Southampton Slave Revolt of 1831: a Compila-*
tion of Source Material (Amherst, Mass., 1971), 308ff.

pose, by telling them something was about to happen that would terminate in fulfilling the great promise that had been made to me. . . . About this time I told these things to a white man, (Etheldred T. Brantley) on whom it had a wonderful effect—and he ceased from his wickedness, and was attacked immediately with a cutaneous eruption, and blood oozed from the pores of his skin, and after praying and fasting nine days, he was healed, and the Spirit appeared to me again, and said, as the Saviour had been baptized so should we be also—and when the white people would not let us be baptised by the church, we went down into the water together, in the sight of many who reviled us, and were baptised by the Spirit—After this I rejoiced greatly, and gave thanks to God. And on the 12th of May, 1828, I heard a loud noise in the heavens, and the Spirit instantly appeared to me and said the Serpent was loosened, and Christ had laid down the yoke he had borne for the sins of men, and that I should take it on and fight against the Serpent, for the time was fast approaching when the first should be last and the last should be first. *QUES.* Do you not find yourself mistaken now? *ANS.* Was not Christ crucified. . . .

Since the commencement of 1830, I had been living with Mr. Joseph Travis, who was to me a kind master, and placed the greatest confidence in me; in fact, I had no cause to complain of his treatment of me. On Saturday evening, the 20th of August, it was agreed between Henry, Hark and myself, to prepare a dinner the next day for the men we expected, and then to concert a plan, as we had not yet determined on any. Hark, on the following morning, brought a pig, and Henry brandy, and being joined by Sam, Nelson, Will and Jack, they prepared in the woods a dinner, where, about three o'clock, I joined them.

Q. Why were you so backward in joining them.

A. The same reason that had caused me not to mix with them for years before.

I saluted them on coming up, and asked Will how came he there, he answered, his life was worth no more than others, and his liberty as dear to him. I asked him if he thought to obtain it? He said he would, or lose his life. This was enough to put him in full confidence. Jack, I knew, was only a tool in the hands of Hark, it was quickly agreed we should commence at home (Mr. J. Travis') on that night, and until we had armed and equipped ourselves, and gathered sufficient force, neither age nor sex was to be spared, (which was invariably adhered to.) We remained at the feast, until about two hours in the night, when we went to the house and found Austin; they all went to the cider press and drank, except myself. On returning to the house Hark went to the door with an axe, for the purpose of breaking it open, as we knew we were strong enough to murder the family, if they were awakened by the noise; but reflecting

that it might create an alarm in the neighborhood, we determined to enter the house secretly, and murder them whilst sleeping. Hark got a ladder and set it against the chimney, on which I ascended, and hoisting a window, entered and came down stairs, unbarred the door, and removed the guns from their places. It was then observed that I must spill the first blood. On which, armed with a hatchet, and accompanied by Will, I entered my master's chamber, it being dark, I could not give a death blow, the hatchet glanced from his head, he sprang from the bed and called his wife, it was his last word, Will laid him dead, with a blow of his axe, and Mrs. Travis shared the same fate, as she lay in bed. . . . From Mrs. Reese's we went to Mrs. Turner's, a mile distant, which we reached about sunrise, on Monday morning. Henry, Austin, and Sam, went to the still, where, finding Mr. Peebles, Austin shot him, and the rest of us went to the house; as we approached, the family discovered us, and shut the door. Vain hope! Will, with one stroke of his axe opened it, and we entered and found Mrs. Turner and Mrs. Newsome in the middle of a room, almost frightened to death. Will immediately killed Mrs. Turner, with one blow of his axe. I took Mrs. Newsome by the hand, and with the sword I had when I was apprehended, I struck her several blows over the head, but not being able to kill her, as the sword was dull. Will turning around and discovering it, dispatched her also. A general destruction of property and search for money and ammunition, always succeeded the murders. . . . Having murdered Mrs. Waller and ten children, we started for Mr. William Williams'—having killed him and two little boys that were there; while engaged in this, Mrs. Williams fled and got some distance from the house, but she was pursued, overtaken, and compelled to get up behind one of the company, who brought her back, and after showing her the mangled body of her lifeless husband, she was told to get down and lay by his side, where she was shot dead. I then started for Mr. Jacob Williams, where the family were murdered—Here we found a young man named Drury, who had come on business with Mr. Williams—he was pursued, overtaken and shot: Mrs. Vaughan was the next place visited—and after murdering the family here, I determined on starting for Jerusalem—Our number amounted now to fifty or sixty, all mounted and armed with guns, axes, swords and clubs. . . .
. [Turner's group was met by a party of white men who had pursued them, and with whom they exchanged shots.] As I saw them re-loading their guns, and more coming up than I saw at first, and several of my bravest men being wounded, the others became panick struck and squandered over the field; the white men pursued and fired on us several times. Hark had his horse shot under him, and I caught another for him as it was running by me; five or six of my men were wounded, but none left on the field; finding myself defeated here I instantly determined to

go through a private way, and cross the Nottoway river at the Cypress Bridge, three miles below Jerusalem, and attack that place in the rear, as I expected they would look for me on the other road, and I had a great desire to get there to procure arms and ammunition. After going a short distance in this private way, accompanied by about twenty men, I overtook two or three who told me the others were dispersed in every direction. After trying in vain to collect a sufficient force to proceed to Jerusalem, I determined to return, as I was sure they would make back to their old neighborhood, where they would join me, make new recruits, and come down again. . . . I concluded Jacob and Nat had been taken, and compelled to betray me. On this I gave up all hope for the present; and on Thursday night after having supplied myself with provisions from Mr. Travis's, I scratched a hole under a pile of fence rails in a field, where I concealed myself for six weeks, never leaving my hiding place but for a few minutes in the dead of night to get water which was very near; thinking by this time I could venture out, I began to go about in the night and eaves drop the houses in the neighborhood; pursuing this course for about a fortnight and gathering little or no intelligence, afraid of speaking to any human being, and returning every morning to my cave before dawn of day. I know not how long I might have led this life, if accident had not betrayed me. . . .

I here proceeded to make some inquiries of [Turner], after assuring him of certain death that awaited him, and that concealment would only bring destruction on the innocent as well as the guilty, of his own color, if he knew of any extensive or concerted plan. His answer was, I do not. When I questioned him as to the insurrection in North Carolina happening about the same time, he denied any knowledge of it; and when I looked him in the face as though I would search his inmost thoughts, he replied, "I see sir, you doubt my word; but can you not think the same ideas, and strange appearances about this time in the heaven's might prompt others, as well as myself, to this undertaking." . . .

A Foreign View:
Charles Dickens on Slavery[17]

Charles Dickens (1812–1870) was a sensation as a novelist, in the United States as well as in Great Britain. In 1842, he was received with acclaim in the States. His American Notes for General Circulation, *published that year, and his novel* Martin Chuzzlewit *(1844), which dealt in part with the American scene, offended portions of American opinion, but were influential in forming impressions of the American character and of slavery in Great Britain.*

In this district, as in all others where slavery sits brooding (I have frequently heard this admitted, even by those who are its warmest advocates), there is an air of ruin and decay abroad which is inseparable from the system. The barns and outhouses are mouldering away; the sheds are patched and half roofless; the log cabins (built in Virginia with external chimneys made of clay or wood) are squalid in the last degree. There is no look of decent comfort anywhere. The miserable stations by the railway side; the great wild woodyards, whence the engine is supplied with fuel; the negro children rolling on the ground before the cabin doors, with dogs and pigs; the biped beasts of burden slinking past: gloom and dejection are upon them all.

In the negro car belonging to the train in which we made this journey were a mother and her children who had just been purchased; the husband and father being left behind with their old owner. The children cried the whole way, and the mother was misery's picture. The champion of Life, Liberty, and the Pursuit of Happiness, who had bought them, rode in the same train; and every time we stopped, got down to see that

[17] Charles Dickens, *American Notes* (London, 1926), 144–148.

they were safe. The black in Sindbad's Travels with one eye in the middle of his forehead which shone like a burning coal, was nature's aristocrat compared with this white gentleman. . . .

The city [Richmond] is the seat of the local parliament of Virginia, and in its shady legislative halls some orators were drowsily holding forth to the hot noonday. By dint of constant repetition, however, these constitutional sights had very little more interest for me than so many parochial vestries; and I was glad to exchange this one for a lounge in a well-arranged public library of some ten thousand volumes, and a visit to a tobacco manufactory, where the workmen were all slaves.

I saw in this place the whole process of picking, rolling, pressing, drying, packing in casks, and branding. All the tobacco thus dealt with was in course of manufacture for chewing; and one would have supposed there was enough in that one storehouse to have filled even the comprehensive jaws of America. In this form the weed looks like the oil-cake on which we fatten cattle, and even without reference to its consequences, is sufficiently uninviting.

Many of the workmen appeared to be strong men, and it is hardly necessary to add that they were all labouring quietly then. After two o'clock in the day they are allowed to sing, a certain number at a time. The hour striking while I was there, some twenty sang a hymn in parts, and sang it by no means ill, pursuing their work meanwhile. A bell rang as I was about to leave, and they all poured forth into a building on the opposite side of the street to dinner. I said several times that I should like to see them at their meal; but as the gentleman to whom I mentioned this desire appeared to be suddenly taken rather deaf, I did not pursue the request. Of their appearance I shall have something to say presently.

On the following day I visited a plantation or farm, of about twelve hundred acres, on the opposite bank of the river. Here again, although I went down with the owner of the estate to the "quarter," as that part of it in which the slaves live is called, I was not invited to enter into any of their huts. All I saw of them was that they were very crazy, wretched cabins, near to which groups of half-naked children basked in the sun or wallowed on the dusty ground. But I believe that this gentleman is a considerate and excellent master, who inherited his fifty slaves, and is neither a buyer nor a seller of human stock; and I am sure, from my own observation and conviction, that he is a kind-hearted, worthy man. . . .

The same decay and gloom that overhang the way by which it is approached, hover above the town of Richmond. There are pretty villas and cheerful houses in its streets, and Nature smiles upon the country round; but jostling its handsome residences, like slavery itself going hand in hand with many lofty virtues, are deplorable tenements, fences unrepaired, walls crumbling into ruinous heaps. Hinting gloomily at things below the surface, these, and many other tokens of the same description, force themselves upon the notice, and are remembered with depressing influence when livelier features are forgotten.

To those who are happily unaccustomed to them, the countenances in the streets and labouring-places, too, are shocking. All men who know that there are laws against instructing slaves, of which the pains and penalties greatly exceed in their amount the fines imposed on those who maim and torture them, must be prepared to find their faces very low in the scale of intellectual expression. But the darkness—not of skin, but mind—which meets the stranger's eye at every turn; the brutalizing and blotting out of all fairer characters traced by Nature's hand, immeasurably outdo his worst belief. That travelled creation of the great satirist's brain, who, fresh from living among horses, peered from a high casement down upon his own kind with trembling horror, was scarcely more repelled and daunted by the sight than those who look upon some of these faces for the first time must surely be.

I left the last of them behind me in the person of a wretched drudge, who, after running to and fro all day till midnight, and moping in his stealthy winks of sleep upon the stairs betweenwhiles, was washing the dark passages at four o'clock in the morning; and went upon my way with a grateful heart that I was not doomed to live where slavery was, and had never had my senses blunted to its wrongs and horrors in a slave-rocked cradle.

Frances Anne Kemble:
An Insider's View of Slavery? [18]

There were remarkably few narratives deploring slavery prepared by slaves or masters; those available were by runaways, abolitionists, or southerners who became northerners and abolitionists, and who could therefore be derogated by slavery defenders as ignorant or malicious. Frances Anne Kemble (1809–1893) came of a famous English stage family, was a successful London actress, came to the United States in 1832, and retired from the stage two years later to marry a distinguished Georgian planter, Pierce Butler. She wrote in 1838–1839 a journal of her experiences as mistress of his plantation and the slavery system she despised, left her husband in 1846, and took up her career in England and the United States. Her journal, as published in 1863, was intended to influence British opinion against recognition of the Confederacy, but it was also received gratefully in the United States North for its exposé of southern cruelty and inhumanity. Franny Kemble's qualifications for assessing slavery have been challenged, but those who responded to her narrative held that her very lack of social sophistication supported the validity of her portrait.

[January, 1839]

I received early this morning a visit from a young Negro called Morris, who came to request permission to be baptized. The master's leave is necessary for this ceremony of acceptance into the bosom of the Christian Church; so all that can be said is, that it is to be hoped the rite itself

[18] Frances Anne Kemble, *Journal of a Residence on a Georgian Plantation in 1838–1839*, edited with an introduction by John A. Scott (New York, 1961), 120–121, 229–231.

may *not* be indispensable for salvation, as, if Mr. [Butler] had thought proper to refuse Morris's petition, he must infallibly have been lost, in spite of his own best wishes to the contrary. I could not, in discoursing with him, perceive that he had any very distinct ideas of the advantages he expected to derive from the ceremony; but perhaps they appeared all the greater for being a little vague. I have seldom seen a more pleasing appearance than that of this young man; his figure was tall and straight, and his face, which was of a perfect oval, rejoiced in the grace, very unusual among his peple, of a fine high forehead, and the much more frequent one of a remarkably gentle and sweet expression. He was, however, jet-black, and certainly did not owe these personal advantages to any mixture in his blood. There is a certain African tribe from which the West Indian slave market is chiefly recruited, who have these same characteristic features, and do not at all present the ignoble and ugly Negro type, so much more commonly seen here. They are a tall, powerful people, with remarkably fine figures, regular features, and a singularly warlike and fierce disposition, in which respect they also differ from the race of Negroes existing on the American plantations. I do not think Morris, however, could have belonged to this tribe, though perhaps Othello did, which would at once settle the difficulties of those commentators who, abiding by Iago's very disagreeable suggestions as to his purely African appearance, are painfully compelled to forego the mitigation of supposing him a Moor and not a Negro. Did I ever tell you of my dining in Boston, at the H——'s, on my first visit to that city, and sitting by Mr. John Quincy Adams, who, talking to me about Desdemona, assured me, with a most serious expression of sincere disgust, that he considered all her misfortunes as a very just judgment upon her for having married a "nigger?" I think, if some ingenious American actor of the present day, bent upon realizing Shakespeare's finest conceptions, with all the advantages of modern enlightenment, could contrive to slip in that opprobrious title, with a true South Carolinian antiabolitionist expression, it might really be made quite a point for Iago, as, for instance, in his first soliloquy—"I hate the nigger," given in proper Charleston or Savannah fashion, I am sure would tell far better than "I hate the Moor." Only think . . . what a very new order of interest the whole tragedy might receive, acted throughout from this standpoint, as the Germans call it in this country, and cailed *Amalgamation, or the Black Bridal.* . . .

I have a mind to transcribe . . . the entries for today recorded in a sort of daybook, where I put down very succinctly the number of people who visit me, their petitions and ailments, and also such special particulars concerning them as seem to me worth recording. You will see how miserable the physical condition of many of these poor creatures is; and their physical condition, it is insisted by those who uphold this evil system, is the only part of it which is prosperous, happy, and compares well with that of Northern laborers. Judge from the details I now send you; and never forget, while reading them, that the people on this plantation are well off, and consider themselves well off, in comparison with the slaves on some of the neighboring estates.

Fanny has had six children; all dead but one. She came to beg to have her work in the field lightened.

Nanny has had three children; two of them are dead. She came to implore that the rule of sending them into the field three weeks after their confinement might be altered.

Leah, Caesar's wife, has had six children; three are dead.

Sophy, Lewis's wife, came to beg for some old linen. She is suffering fearfully; has had ten children; five of them are dead. The principal favor she asked was a piece of meat, which I gave her.

Sally, Scipio's wife, has had two miscarriages and three children born, one of whom is dead. She came complaining of incessant pain and weakness in her back. This woman was a mulatto daughter of a slave called Sophy, by a white man of the name of Walker, who visited the plantation.

Charlotte, Renty's wife, had had two miscarriages, and was with child again. She was almost crippled with rheumatism, and showed me a pair of poor swollen knees that made my heart ache. I have promised her a pair of flannel trousers, which I must forthwith set about making. . . .

Sukey, Bush's wife, only came to pay her respects. She had had four miscarriages; had brought eleven children into the world, five of whom are dead.

Molly, Quambo's wife, also came to see me. Hers was the best account I have yet received; she had had nine children, and six of them were still alive.

This is only the entry for today, in my diary, of the people's complaints and visits. Can you conceive a more wretched picture than that which it exhibits of the conditions under which these women live? . . .

There was hardly one of these women, as you will see by the details I have noted of their ailments, who might not have been a candidate for a bed in a hospital, and they had come to me after working all day in the fields.

William Wells Brown:
Pictures of Slave Life[19]

*In 1834, a slave named William Sanford (1815–1884), born in Kentucky
and transported to Missouri, made his escape to freedom, following a life of
travel and varied labors. He changed his name to William Wells Brown, in
tribute to an Ohio benefactor, and took up residence in Cleveland, where he
aided fugitive slaves escaping to Canada. In 1844 he became an active abolitionist. Three years later, he published in Boston his* Narrative of William
W. Brown, a Fugitive Slave. *He was disturbed by a panorama of the Mississippi River which he believed gave a deceptively mild view of the slavery
institution. Brown prepared an illustrated lecture on its reality as he knew it,
and offered it on platforms in Great Britain, where he was well received. He
was also persuaded to permit friends to purchase his freedom; he had turned
down earlier opportunities on grounds that he could not recognize property
rights in his person. Brown was a pioneer Negro author, and his* Clotel; or
the President's Daughter *(1853) is a pioneer Negro novel.*

View Second

*Two Gangs of Slaves Chained and on their way to the Market—Cruel Sepa-
ration of a Mother from her Child—White Slaves.*

We have now before us a gang of Slaves on their way to the City of
Washington. You see that they are chained together. The white men in
the foreground of the view are the agents of the notorious Franklin and
Armfield, of Washington, one of the largest slave-dealing houses in the

[19] *A Description of William Wells Brown's Original Panoramic Views of the
Scenes in the Life of an American Slave, from His Birth in Slavery to His
Death or His Escape to His First Home of Freedom on British Soil* (Lon-
don [, 1849]), n.p.

United States. The house before us is an Inn. The agents have been in different directions purchasing slaves, and have joined their gangs together in this place.

On the right of you, you see a woman who will not go on, and a slave in the act of taking away her young child. She has been separated from it, and they are now whipping her to make her proceed without it.

You readily recognise two Slaves as being nearly white.

It is not uncommon to see slaves as white as their masters, and a great deal better-looking, chained and driven as the beasts of the field.

It was in reference to a scene like this, which is one of continual occurrence in America, that the poet Whittier wrote the following spirited lines:—

> "What, ho! our countrymen in chains!
>   The whip on Woman's shrinking flesh!
> Our soil yet reddening with the stains
>   Caught from her scourging, warm and fresh!
>
> What! mothers from their children driven!
>   What! God's own image bought and sold!
> *Americans* to market driven,
>   And bartered, like the brutes, for gold!"

View Eleventh

Slaves Burying their Dead at Night by Torchlight.

The view now before us needs little or no explanation. You will see, at a glance, that it is a funeral. Slaves are not permitted to bury their dead during the day, except in some of the better portions of Virginia, Kentucky, and Maryland.

View Seventeenth

St. Louis—Second Scene in the Life of WILLIAM WELLS BROWN— *Boat on Fire.*

We have here a view of the city of St. Louis, Missouri, by moonlight. This is one of the most important inland towns in the United States, being at the head of navigation of the great Mississippi. By the aid of moonlight, and the light from the boat on fire, we are enabled to see some of the prominent buildings in the city from the Illinois shore, where we may now imagine ourselves to stand. The dome of the large Presbyterian Chapel, the Planters' Hotel, the Markethouse, and the

Town or City Hall, are to be seen. The steamboat in the foreground of the view is the Chester, commanded by Capt. Enoch Price. The boat is just leaving St. Louis for New Orleans. The two persons in the small boat just astern of the Chester, are the writer and his mother, attempting to escape from Slavery. . . . The boat on fire is a flat boat; or, as they are called on the Mississippi, "broad horns." These boats are seen in great numbers floating down the rivers Ohio and Mississippi. With the exception of an oar at each end, by means of which they are steered, they are entirely at the mercy of the current of the river. These boats are usually laden with pork, flour, cattle, and corn, and generally lie by at night. The man in the water, is one who has escaped from the burning boat.

William Still:
Chronicles of Enslavement[20]

The slavery institution inevitably involved great numbers of distinguished persons who had owned slaves, or in some fashion had been involved in the workings of slavery. Thus, William Wells Brown's novel Clotel *confirmed the unsubstantiated rumor that Thomas Jefferson had had a child by a Negro slave, whom he had sold. William Still's collection of "Facts, Authentic Narratives, Letters, &c." relating to fugitive slave efforts included many references illuminating pages from the history of slavery.*

EX-PRESIDENT TYLER'S HOUSEHOLD LOSES
AN ARISTOCRATIC "ARTICLE"

James Hambleton Christian is a remarkable specimen of the "well fed, &c." In talking with him relative to his life as a slave, he said very promptly, "I have always been treated well; if I only have half as good times in the North as I have had in the South, I shall be perfectly satisfied. Any time I desired spending money, five or ten dollars were no object." At times, James had borrowed of his master, one, two, and three hundred dollars, to loan out to some of his friends. With regard to apparel and jewelry, he had worn the best, as an every-day adornment. With regard to food also, he had fared as well as heart could wish, with abundance of leisure time at his command. His deportment was certainly very refined and gentlemanly. About fifty per cent. of Anglo-Saxon blood was visible in his features and his hair, which gave him no inconsiderable claim to sympathy and care. He had been to William and Mary's College in his younger days, to wait on young master James B. C., where, through the kindness of some of the students he had picked

[20] William Still, *The Underground Railroad* (Philadelphia, 1872), 69–70.

up a trifling amount of book learning. To be brief, this man was born the slave of old Major Christian, on the Glen Plantation, Charles City county, Va. The Christians were wealthy and owned many slaves, and belonged in reality to the F.F.V's. On the death of the old Major, James fell into the hands of his son, Judge Christian, who was executor to his father's estate. Subsequently he fell into the hands of one of the Judge's sisters, Mrs. John Tyler (wife of Ex-President Tyler), and then he became a member of the President's domestic household, was at the White House, under the President, from 1841 to 1845. Though but very young at that time, James was only fit for training in the arts, science, and mystery of waiting, in which profession, much pains were taken to qualify him completely for his calling.

After a lapse of time; his mistress died. According to her request, after this event, James and his old mother were handed over to her nephew, William H. Christian, Esq., a merchant of Richmond. From this gentleman, James had the folly to flee.

Passing hurriedly over interesting details, received from him respecting his remarkable history, two or three more incidents too good to omit must suffice.

"How did you like Mr. Tyler?" said an inquisitive member of the Vigilance Committee. "I didn't like Mr. Tyler much," was the reply. "Why?" again inquired the member of the Committee. "Because Mr. Tyler was a poor man. I never did like poor people. I didn't like him marrying into our family, who were considered very far Tyler's superiors." "On the plantation," he said, "Tyler was a very cross man, and treated the servants very cruelly; but the house servants were treated much better, owing to their having belonged to his wife, who protected them from persecution, as they had been favorite servants in her father's family." James estimated that "Tyler got about thirty-five thousand dollars and twenty-nine slaves, young and old, by his wife."

What prompted James to leave such pleasant quarters? It was this: He had become enamored of a young and respectable free girl in Richmond with whom he could not be united in marriage solely because he was a slave and did not own himself. The frequent sad separations of such married couples (where one or the other was a slave) could not be overlooked; consequently, the poor fellow concluded that he would stand a better chance of gaining his object in Canada than by remaining in Virginia. So he began to feel that he might himself be sold some day, and thus the resolution came home to him very forcibly to make tracks for Canada.

In speaking of the good treatment he had always met with, a member of the Committee remarked, "You must be akin to some one of your master's family?" To which he replied, "I am Christian's son." Unques-

tionably this passenger was one of that happy class so commonly referred to by apologists for the "Patriarchal Institution." The Committee,
feeling a deep interest in his story, and desiring great success to him in
his Underground efforts to get rid of slavery, and at the same time pos-
sess himself of his affianced, made him heartily welcome, feeling assured
that the struggles and hardships he had submitted to in escaping, as well
as the luxuries he was leaving behind, were nothing to be compared with
the blessings of liberty and a free wife in Canada.

Harriet Beecher Stowe:
The Sale of Uncle Tom[21]

The story of Uncle Tom's Cabin *(1852), its creation and effect, is one of the epic events of pre-Civil War history. The excitement it caused North and South was unprecedented, this despite the steady piling up of dramatic abolitionist confrontations, fugitive slave narratives, tense political crises, and bloody riots. In some fashion Mrs. Stowe's prose brought into focus the feelings and attitudes of a majority of northerners, and in doing so congealed those of their antagonists to the south. Mrs. Stowe (1811–1896) made no visit to New Orleans; her experience with the South was limited to parts of Kentucky, which she visited while living in Cincinnati, Ohio. Yet the many scenes of plantation life depicted in her tale stood out as authentic to a national audience which had for years been fed vivid tales of life as it was said to be lived in the South. Although "Uncle Tom" himself became stereotyped as servile and contemptible (to Negro spokesmen, as well as whites), it should be noted that he was, as originally depicted, dignified, courageous, superior to his oppressors, and an altogether honorable figure.*

Beneath a splendid dome were men of all nations, moving to and fro over the marble *pavé*. On every side of the circular were little tribunes, or stations, for the use of speakers and auctioneers. Two of these, on opposite sides of the area, were now occupied by brilliant and talented gentlemen, enthusiastically forcing up, in English and French commingled, the bids of connoisseurs in their various wares. A third one, on the other side, still unoccupied, was surrounded by a group waiting the moment of sale to begin. And here we may recognise the St. Clare servants, Tom,

[21] Harriet Beecher Stowe, *Uncle Tom's Cabin*, intro. by Van Wyck Brooks (London, 1966 ed.), 332–335.

Adolph, and others; and there, too, Susan and Emmeline, awaiting their turn, with anxious and dejected faces. Various spectators, intending to purchase, or not to purchase, as the case might be, gathered around the group, handling, examining, and commenting on their various points and faces, with the same freedom that a set of jockeys discuss the merits of a horse.

"Holloa, Alf! what brings you here?" said a young exquisite, slapping the shoulder of a sprucely dressed young man, who was examining Adolph through an eyeglass.

"Well, I was wanting a valet, and I heard that St. Clare's lot was going. I thought I'd just look at his"——

"Catch me ever buying any of St. Clare's people! Spoilt niggers, every one! Impudent as the devil!" said the other.

"Never fear that!" said the first. "If I get 'em, I'll soon have their airs out of them; they'll soon find that they've another kind of master to deal with than Monsieur St. Clare. 'Pon my word, I'll buy that fellow. I like the shape of him."

"You'll find it'll take all you've got to keep him. He's deucedly extravagant!"

"Yes, but my lord will find that he *can't* be extravagant with *me*. Just let him be sent to the calaboose a few times, and thoroughly dressed down! I'll tell you if it don't bring him to a sense of his ways! Oh, I'll reform him, up hill and down—you'll see! I buy him, that's flat!"

Tom had been standing wistfully examining the multitude of faces thronging around him for one whom he would wish to call master; and if you should ever be under the necessity, sir, of selecting out of two hundred men one who was to become your absolute owner and disposer, you would perhaps realise, just as Tom did, how few there were that you would feel at all comfortable in being made over to. Tom saw abundance of men, great, burly, gruff men; little, chirping, dried men; long-favoured, lank, hard men; and every variety of stubbed-looking, commonplace men, who pick up their fellow-men as one picks up chips, putting them into the fire or a basket with equal unconcern, according to their convenience; but he saw no St. Clare.

A little before the sale commenced, a short, broad, muscular man, in a checked shirt considerably open at the bosom, and pantaloons much the worse for dirt and wear, elbowed his way through the crowd, like one who is going actively into a business; and, coming up to the group, began to examine them systematically. From the moment that Tom saw him approaching, he felt an immediate and revolting horror at him, that increased as he came near. He was evidently, though short, of gigantic strength. His round, bullet head, large, light-grey eyes, with their shaggy, sandy eyebrows, and stiff, wiry, sunburnt hair, were rather unprepossess-

ing items, it is to be confessed; his large, coarse mouth was distended
with tobacco, the juice of which, from time to time, he ejected from him
with great decision and explosive force; his hands were immensely large,
hairy, sunburnt, freckled, and very dirty, and garnished with long nails,
in a very foul condition. This man proceeded to a very free personal examination of the lot. He seized Tom by the jaw, and pulled open his
mouth to inspect his teeth; made him strip up his sleeve, to show his
muscle; turned him round, made him jump and spring, to show his
paces.

"Where was you raised?" he added briefly to these investigations.

"In Kintuck, mas'r," said Tom, looking about as if for deliverance.

"What have you done?"

"Had care of mas'r's farm," said Tom.

"Likely story!" said the other shortly, as he passed on. He paused a
moment before Dolph; then spitting a discharge of tobacco-juice on his
well-blacked boots, and giving a contemptuous umph, he walked on.
Again he stopped before Susan and Emmeline. He put out his heavy,
dirty hand, and drew the girl towards him; passed it over her neck and
bust, felt her arms, looked at her teeth, and then pushed her back against
her mother, whose patient face showed the suffering she had been going
through at every motion of the hideous stranger.

The girl was frightened, and began to cry.

"Stop that, you minx!" said the salesman; "no whimpering here, the
sale is going to begin." And accordingly the sale begun.

Adolph was knocked off at a good sum, to the young gentleman who
had previously stated his intention of buying him; and the other servants
of the St. Clare lot went to various bidders.

"Now, up with you, boy! d'ye hear?" said the auctioneer to Tom.

Tom stepped upon the block, gave a few anxious looks round; all
seemed mingled in a common, indistinct noise—the clatter of the salesman crying off his qualifications in French and English, the quick fire of
French and English bids; and almost in a moment came the final thump
of the hammer, and the clear ring on the last syllable of the word *"dollars,"* as the auctioneer announced his price, and Tom was made over.
He had a master!

He was pushed from the block; the short, bullet-headed man, seizing
him roughly by the shoulder, pushed him to one side, saying, in a harsh
voice, "Stand there, *you!*"

Tom hardly realised anything; but still the bidding went on—rattling,
clattering, now French, now English. Down goes the hammer again,—
Susan is sold. She goes down from the block, stops, looks wistfully back;
her daughter stretches her hands towards her. She looks with agony in
the face of the man who has bought her—a respectable middle-aged
man, of benevolent countenance.

"O mas'r, please do buy my daughter!"

"I'd like to, but I'm afraid I can't afford it," said the gentleman, looking with painful interest as the young girl mounted the block, and looked around her with a frightened and timid glance.

The blood flushes painfully in her otherwise colourless cheek, her eyes have a feverish fire, and her mother groans to see that she looks more beautiful than she ever saw her before. The auctioneer sees his advantage, and expatiates volubly in mingled French and English, and bids rise in rapid succession.

"I'll do anything in reason," said the benevolent-looking gentleman, pressing in, and joining with the bids. In a few moments they have run beyond his purse. He is silent; the auctioneer grows warmer; but bids gradually drop off. It lies now between an aristocratic old citizen and our bullet-headed acquaintance. The citizen bids for a few turns, contemptuously measuring his opponent; but the bullet-head has the advantage over him, both in obstinacy and concealed length of purse, and the controversy lasts but a moment; the hammer falls—he has got the girl, body and soul, unless God help her!

Her master is Mr. Legree who owns a cotton plantation on the Red River. She is pushed along in the same lot with Tom and two other men, and goes off, weeping as she goes.

The benevolent gentleman is sorry; but then the thing happens every day! One sees girls and mothers crying at these sales *always!* it can't be helped, etc.; and he walks off with his acquisition in another direction.

Two days after the lawyer of the Christian firm of B. and Co., New York, sent on their money to them. On the reverse of that draft, so obtained, let them write these words of the great Paymaster, to whom they shall make up their account in a future day:—*"When he maketh inquisition for blood, he forgetteth not the cry of the humble!"*

The Border States: A Slave's Wedding[22]

Full understanding of the psychology of slaveholders and slaves in the several states affected would have demanded the insight of a master novelist, such as William Faulkner later provided for his native Mississippi. It is certain that there were differences between attitudes fostered in the Border States and those developed farther south. The following account of a slave's wedding was written by the daughter of a slaveholder, formerly of Kentucky, now practicing law and plantation arts in western Missouri, close to the Kansas border.

The next morning I looked at the sideboard as I did as soon as I entered the dining room. It was piled higher than I had ever seen it with cutout trousers and jackets. At night the sideboard bore finished clothes; in the morning cut-out ones. I played to myself that the garments unmade themselves at night, just as Penelope had unraveled her weaving. I had barely finished my breakfast when Mother said, "Manie, we will not wait until eight o'clock. We'll have your lesson right away. Betsey is going to marry Jo Burt." I wanted to shout, "I knew it, I knew it!" I had seen Aunt Lucy's girl walking with the half-white Jo, but did not interrupt.

Mother was saying that she had to make new suits for Lucy's family to wear to the wedding. Too, Betsey must have a suitable outfit, and her sister Letty a pretty dress. "I had thought to make out the rest of this summer without sewing for you and Julia," Mother added. "But your dresses are too short with guests in the house. Your father is bound to hire a sewing woman. I am going to do all I can so as not to have help employed any longer than necessary."

[22] Manie Morgan, *The New Stars: Life and Labor in Old Missouri,* as arranged by Jennie A. Morgan, ed. Louis Filler (Yellow Springs, Ohio, 1949), 11–15.

Letty was brought into the room to wax the threads, knot the ends, and thread needles. Mother did not rise from her chair, but stitched steadily. At the dinner table, she said, "Lucy, Manie's chatter makes me nervous. Take charge of her until this rush of sewing is over." I hoped I would get down to the negro quarters and away from the big house.

That afternoon Aunt Lucy spread the parlor carpet, which she had washed in the forenoon, over a thick layer of straw, and she and I tramped about on it. When I fell down and giggled, she giggled with me. We soon flattened the straw, and then Aunt Lucy tacked the carpet down, having me hand her each tack and asking me all the time (very low so as not to disturb Mother at her sewing in the next room) if she had it stretched straight. . . .

William Estis (Uncle Bill) arrived from Lexington, Kentucky, for the wedding of his daughter a week early. Our slaves' surname was Estis, though most slaves, just as Jo Burt did, took the name of their owner. Uncle Bill was a free negro. His master had emancipated all his slaves and had given each a cabin and five acres of ground. Uncle Bill went to Lexington each spring to plant tobacco and came back to our place each fall after he had marketed the cigars he had made. His neighbors tended his crops while he came to the wedding. Uncle Bill mowed the lawn with a scythe and had Aunt Lucy and me look to see that "there are no bumps left this time." When I noticed one that Aunt Lucy had not, he said, "Thank you, Mis' Manie."

My mother taught me my lessons and Julia practiced her music. The rest of the day from early morning until eight o'clock at night, Mother, Aunt Angeline, and a sewing woman worked. They made the jackets and trousers of the negro men and boys first to have them off hands, and too, the dress materials had had to be ordered. We knew Mother's step-brother, William Page of St. Louis, would hurry the order Father had telegraphed, but it came even sooner than we expected. There was one box marked, "For the Bride," and Mother gave it to Betsey, saying, "You can surprise us." . . .

The wedding was set for eight o'clock. Father took charge. The couple were to stand in front of the door leading from the parlor into the dining room. The divans and chairs were put near this door and facing it. These made seats for the white people, and the blacks would stand in the rear.

Mr. and Mrs. Burt and the Smith family sat with us on the divans. Mrs. Burt had a green dress with yellow roses as large as saucers. Aunt Angeline wore a solid pink dress, very plain, with a fine lace collar and cameo pin. Pink was pretty with her smooth dark hair. Mrs. Burt had wavy yellow hair. Mother's dress was a black lawn with peacocks on it, the color of the real birds and almost as large. When the wind blew her skirt about, I saw a whole bird. The waist was a bird without a tail. The men wore black broadcloth suits and ruffled shirts. My father's dark hair curled from his smooth, beardless face like that of the poet Shelley.

I think our black folks had been waiting, for they came in after the Burts and Smiths. Aunt Lucy and Uncle Bill walked at the head of their family. They were side by side, but Aunt Lucy seemed ahead. She had on her black alpaca, which she wore only to funerals. She and Uncle Bill waited at the door while their fourteen broad-shouldered sons, in their shining new shoes and creaseless new suits, walked by. Their coats were buttoned over their chests to the throat like jackets. The little boys, Jo and Josh, wore only long linen shirts, new and smooth, and were barefoot. Letty's eyes were soft and shining in her bony face. The negro guests filled the room. The negro preacher had an unbleached linen suit, but his coat was made like white folks' coats, and he wore a stiff shirt and collar, and a necktie.

At a sign from the preacher Julia played the new wedding march, and Jo and Betsey came from the guest bedroom. An audible sigh went up from Betsey's little brothers and Letty, and I fear from me, at the sight of her. Her round face looked childish. Her chocolate brown skin was pretty against her white, lacy veil, and so were her brown arms clasping the scarlet roses. Her hair looked soft and black against the orange blossoms. Jo Burt wore white linen pants, a white shirt, a black tie, and a white coat. His hair was cut short. His homely yellow face was intelligent and kind.

As I think back, I again hear the minister say, "In the presence of God," and see the solemn faces of Jo and Betsey. I know that there were other words, but those were all that I heard. I probably daydreamed between times with myself as Betsey. I thought it was strange for the minister to tell grown-ups to do things like "join your hands." I remember how the solemnity left Jo's face when the minister asked if he would take Betsey "for better or worse—until death doth you part." It became warm and happy with love as he said, "I do." Betsey smiled when she answered, "I do," to the same question. Soon the minister was shaking hands with Jo and Betsey, and I heard him say, "Mrs. Burt." . . .

READING NO. **23**

Slavery for Northerners: A Proposal[23]

Over the antislavery controversy rested the possibility that successful efforts might be made to reintroduce slavery into northern territories, and eventually throughout the Union. Kansas offered a particularly attractive target for the innovation because it was adjacent to a slaveholding state (Missouri), had attracted Free Soil settlers many of whom had no regard for Negroes, and if granted slavery, could furnish a precedent for similar actions elsewhere. The following was abstracted from an 1854 Report Made to the Platte County Self-Defensive Association, *Platte being a Missouri county which bordered on Kansas. Daniel R. Goodloe (1814–1902), who responded to the challenge, was a North Carolinian who repudiated slavery and became a founder of the Republican Party.*

In obedience to a resolution adopted by the Platte County Self-Defensive Association, we proceed to lay before the public the immediate causes which led to the formation of the Association; to explain its purposes, and to suggest the means, which seem to us proper to be adopted by the citizens of the slaveholding States, to defeat the designs of the abolitionists. . . .

Admit it an evil, how is it to be mitigated? No immediate cure is practicable; temporary alleviation only can be given. We propose now to alleviate it, if it be an evil; to extend its benefits, if it be a blessing.

To extend the limits, open a wider field for the employment of slaves, is, of all others, the remedy for the evil, if it be an evil; the most effectual to extend its benefits, if it be a blessing.

[23] *Information for the People. Two Tracts for the Times. The One Entitled "Negro-Slavery, No Evil:" the Other, an Answer to the Inquiry "Is It Expedient to Introduce Slavery into Kanzas?" by D. R. Goodloe, of North Carolina. Republished by the N[ew] E[ngland] Emigrant Aid Co.* (Boston, 1855), 3, 34.

By this, not one is added to the number of the slaves; on the contrary, the number is thus most likely to diminish. The inducement which more than all others leads the master to liberate his slave, is the affection of the master. To the growth of that affection the good conduct of the slave, intimate and familiar intercourse with the master, the sympathy of association mainly conduce. The master does not liberate his slave from hatred, but from love; from a desire to benefit him, as a reward for fidelity.

Where a master is the owner of but few slaves, is personally associated with each of them, it is natural that he should feel a deeper interest in them, a more lively attachment for them, than where, by their very numbers, they are excluded from his presence; are as strangers to him; of necessity, too often subjected to the control of another. Such is the difference in the attachment of the employer to his domestic "help," his housekeeper, his chambermaid, the servants of his household, and to those of the field or the factory.

By opening a wider field for the employment of slaves, they are divided into smaller parties; the number of owners increased; the proportion of slaves diminished; a closer intimacy necessarily arises between them; affection springs up, and liberty becomes the reward of fidelity.

This same cause equally contributes to the advancement of the moral and physical condition of the slave; tends to fit him for liberty. The watchful eye of the master is brought more closely to bear, and he is stimulated by affection to guard and protect his slave with a kinder care. Not crowded together, they are of necessity healthier; their numbers meet for social intercourse, not such as to corrupt by association, with their masters' example constantly before them, their moral condition is equally improved.

All, then, who feel for the slave, not mock but real sympathy, should unite to extend the limits within which they may be employed. . . .

The Proslavery Answer
to British Criticism[24]

Southern apologists for slavery veered between identifying their civiliza-
tion with that of the English country gentleman and resenting British crit-
icism of slavery and its support of American abolitionists who collected funds
abroad in furtherance of their States-side activities. Proslavery arguments
drew strength from Parliamentary reports describing the pitiful lives of fac-
tory, mine, and other classes of laborers. The White Slaves of England, *by*
John C. Cobden, was lavish in its sympathy for these oppressed elements,
quoting copiously from detailed accounts of the conditions they endured, and
contrasting their lot with the allegedly happier and more secure lives of
American slaves. The book's "twelve spirited illustrations" depicted women
and children at the looms, a young girl dragging a coal cart through a nar-
row seam underground, and other scenes of like character. John C. Cobden
has not been identified.

Mr. Mayhew, in his "London Labour and the London Poor," shows
that a large number of the vagrants of London and other English cities,
are young persons who have been servants, and have run away in consequence of ill-treatment. Rather than be constantly treated as slaves, the
boys prefer to be vagabonds and the girls prostitutes. They then enjoy a
wild kind of freedom, which, with all its filth and vice, has some share of
pleasure, unknown to those who move at the beck of a master or mistress, and live in constant dread of the rod.

In those countries where society is untainted with aristocracy, the

[24] John C. Cobden, *The White Slaves of England, Compiled from Official
Documents* (Auburn and Buffalo, N.Y., and Cincinnati, 1853), 376–377,
494–496.

servant when performing duties is respected as a human being—with a mind to think and a heart to feel—one to be reprimanded or discharged from service for neglect or positive wrong, but never beaten as a soulless beast. In England, the servant, to hold a place, must be a most abject, cringing, and submissive slave. In some countries, the taint of negro blood keeps a man always in the position of an inferior. In England, the man of "serf blood," though he be a Celt or Saxon, is ever treated as a hind by the man of "noble blood;" and the possession of this same "noble blood" justifies the most infamous scoundrel in treating his domestics, not only with contempt, but positive cruelty. Americans have been charged with having an undying horror of the negro taint. In England, the *common* blood is just as steadily abhorred by the dominant class. The slavery of servants—their hopeless, abject, and demoralizing condition—is the result, direct and unmistakable, of the existence of the aristocracy. . . .

The crime of England lies in maintaining the slavery of a barbarous age in the middle of the nineteenth century; in keeping her slaves in physical misery, mental darkness, moral depravity, and heathenism; in carrying fire and sword into some of the loveliest regions of the earth, in order to gratify that thirst for wealth and dominion ever characteristic of an aristocracy; in forcing her slaves in India to cultivate poison, and her weak neighbours of China to buy it; in plundering and oppressing the people of all her colonies; in concentrating the wealth of the United Kingdom and the dependencies in the purses of a few persons, and thus dooming all others beneath her iron rule to constant, exhausting, and unrewarded toil! We arraign her before the tribunal of justice and humanity, as the most powerful and destructive of tyrannies; as the author of Ireland's miseries, and a course of action toward that island compared with which the dismemberment of Poland was merciful; as the remorseless conqueror of the Hindoos; as a government so oppressive that her people are flying by thousands to the shores of America to escape its inflictions! . . .

We think it not difficult to show that England is the best friend of slavery, while professing an aversion to it, and dictating to other governments to strive for its abolition. At an enormous expense, she maintains men-of-war upon the coast of Africa, with the object of suppressing the trade in negro slaves. This expense her white slaves are taxed to pay; while the men-of-war have not only not suppressed the slave-trade, but have doubled its horrors, by compelling the slave-traders to inflict new tortures upon the negroes they capture and conceal. In the mean time, the government is doing all in its power to impoverish and enslave (for the slavery of a people follows its poverty) the more intelligent races of the world. England prides herself upon her efforts to destroy the trade in African savages and chattel slavery. Her philanthropy is all black; miserable wretches with pale faces have no claims upon her assisting hand; and she refuses to recognise the only kind of slavery by which masters are necessitated to provide well for their slaves, while she enforces that system which starves them! England is the best friend of the most destructive species of slavery, and has extended it over tens of millions of human beings.

Henry Clay: What Is to Be Done? [25]

Abraham Lincoln considered Henry Clay (1777–1852) his ideal of what an American statesman should be, and strove to emulate Clay's national view and moderation. Clay held himself to be antislavery in sentiment. He had been one of the major supporters of the American Colonization Society, and he honored Free Soil. Yet his failure to stand firmly for antislavery measures in 1844 were to cost him the support of the relatively few abolitionists, and thereby lose him New York's electoral votes and the Presidency, which thus fell to James K. Polk, a firm proslavery figure. Clay's hopes for a peaceful solution to the dilemmas posed by slavery—hopes expressed in the following letter, written in 1842—were shared by a majority of Americans.

I regard the existence of slavery as an evil. I regret it, and wish that there was not one slave in the United States.

But it is an evil which, while it affects the States only, or principally, where it abounds, each State within which it is situated is the exclusive judge of what is best to be done with it, and no other State has a right to interfere in it. Kentucky has no right to interfere with the slavery of Virginia, and Ohio has no right to interfere with it in either. . . .

Although I believe slavery to be an evil, I regard it as a far less evil than would arise out of an immediate emancipation of the slaves of the United States, and their remaining here mixed up in our communities. In such a contingency, I believe that a bloody civil war would ensue, which would terminate only by the extinction of the black race. . . .

I have regretted extremely the agitation of abolition in the free States. It has done no good, but harm. It will do no good. The great body of Abolitionists, like the great mass of every party, I have no doubt, is hon-

---

[25] Calvin Colton, ed., *The Private Correspondence of Henry Clay* (New York, 1855), 463–466.

est, sincere, and humane. Their leaders deceive them, and will endeavor to profit by them. They will seek to ride into public office, and to snatch public honor, upon the delusions which they propagate.

Abolition is a delusion which can not last. It is impossible it should endure. What is it? In pursuit of a principle—a great principle, if you please, it undertakes to tread down and trample in the dust all opposing principles, however sacred. It sets up the right of the people of one State to dictate to the people of other States. It arrays State against State. To make the black man free, it would virtually enslave the white man. With a single idea some of its partisans rush on blindly, regardless of all consequences. They have dared even to threaten our glorious Union with dissolution. And suppose that unhallowed object achieved, would it emancipate the slaves? What is their next step? Is it to light up a war between the dissevered parts of the Union, and through blood, devastation, and conflagration, to march forward to emancipation? Are they at all sure that through such diabolical means they would be able finally to arrive at their object? . . .

But what is ultimately to become of slavery? asks the impatient Abolitionist. I can not tell him with any certainty. I have no doubt that the merciful Providence, which permitted its introduction into our country against the wishes of our ancestors, will, according to His own good pleasure and time, provide for its mitigation or termination.

In the mean time, we have had much to encourage us. Our Revolution led to the cessation of the African slave trade with the United States. It altogether ceased in 1808. Many States emancipated their slaves, not by the perilous process of an immediate liberation, but by the gradual and cautious proceeding of a slow and regulated emancipation, liberating the offspring at mature age, and leaving the parents in slavery; thus making preparation for the proper use of the liberty which their children were to enjoy. Every where a spirit of humanity was, more and more, infusing itself into the laws for the regulation of the treatment of slaves, until it was checked, in some places, by the agitation of Abolition. Some States, where the proportion of slaves was not very great in comparison with the whites, were beginning seriously to think about the practicability of a gradual emancipation within their limits, but they, too, have been checked by the intemperate zeal of Abolitionists. The feasibility of African colonization has been demonstrated, and the Society, with its limited means, has been quietly prosecuting its noble object.

By some of the means indicated, and others hidden from our view, by an all-wise Providence, we may cherish the hope that, if violent Abolitionists will cease stirring up strife and agitating the passions, we may ultimately alleviate the evils, if not eradicate the existence of slavery in our land.

The generation that established our independence achieved a great and glorious work. Succeeding generations have accomplished much in advancing the growth, the power, and the greatness of this nation. We must leave some things to posterity, and among others the task of making adequate provision for the institution of Slavery.

In spite of slavery, our arms triumphed in the revolutionary struggle. And it is not too much to assert that, if Abolition had developed itself then, as it since has done, we should have failed. We should have been unable to form the Confederation, or subsequently to have adopted the present Constitution. In spite of slavery, we were successful in the second war with Great Britain. And in neither war, it is a gratifying historical fact, was the enemy able, by all his arts of seduction, to withdraw many slaves from their fidelity. In spite of slavery, we have moved onward in our march to power and greatness, augmenting our population, in a period only co-extensive with that of my own life, from two and a half to seventeen millions.

Frederick Douglass on
"The Slavery Party" [26]

The view that slavery might evolve into more modern permutations of social and labor relations had long kept the antislavery feelings of Americans North and South from maturing into firmer abolitionist convictions. When it became clear that the dominant elements of southern social and political life regarded slavery not as a regrettable episode in national life but as a "positive good," points of view crystallized which threatened a national consensus. Frederick Douglass in 1853, at the anniversary meeting of the American and Foreign Anti-Slavery Society in New York, spelled out the southern program for his own partisans.

It is evident that there is in this country a purely slavery party, a party which exists for no other earthly purpose but to promote the interest of slavery. It is known by no particular name, and has assumed no definite shape, but its branches reach far and wide in church and state. This shapeless and nameless party is not intangible in other and more important respects. It has a fixed, definite, and comprehensive policy towards the whole free colored population of the United States. I understand that policy to comprehend: First, the complete suppression of all Anti-Slavery discussion; second, the expulsion of the entire free people of the United States; third, the nationalization of slavery; fourth, guarantees for the endless perpetuation of slavery and its extension over Mexico and Central America. Sir, these objects are forcibly presented to us in the stern logic of passing events, and in all the facts that have been before us during the last three years. The country has been and is dividing on these grand issues. Old party ties are broken. Like is finding its like on both sides of these issues, and the great battle is at hand. . . .

[26] Frederick Douglass, *Life and Times* . . . (New York, 1941), 327–330.

The key-stone to the arch of this grand union of forces of the slave party is the so-called Compromise of 1850. In that measure we have all the objects of our slaveholding policy specified. It is, sir, favorable to this view of the situation, that the Whig party and the Democratic party bent lower, sunk deeper, and strained harder in their conventions, preparatory to the late presidential election, to meet the demands of slavery. Never did parties come before the Northern people with propositions of such undisguised contempt for the moral sentiment and religious ideas of that people. They dared to ask them to unite with them in a war upon free speech, upon conscience, and to drive the Almighty presence from the councils of the nation. Resting their platforms upon the fugitive slave bill, they have boldly asked this people for political power to execute its horrible and hell-black provisions. . . .

While this kind of legislation is going on in the States, a pro-slavery political board of health is being established at Washington. Senators Hale, Chase, and Sumner are robbed of their Senatorial rights and dignity as representatives of sovereign States, because they have refused to be inoculated with the pro-slavery virus of the times. Among the services that a Senator is expected to perform are many that can only be done efficiently by those acting as members of important committees, and the slave power in the Senate, in saying to these honorable Senators, you shall not serve on the committees of this body, took the responsibility of insulting and robbing the States which have sent them there. It is an attempt at Washington to decide for the States who the States shall send to the Senate. . . .

Let attention now be called to the social influences operating and co-operating with the slave power of the time and designed to promote all its malign objects. We see here the black man attacked in his most vital interests: prejudice and hate are systematically excited against him. The wrath of other laborers is stirred up against him. The Irish, who, at home, readily sympathize with the oppressed everywhere, are instantly taught when they step upon our soil to hate and despise the Negro. They are taught to believe that he eats the bread that belongs to them. The cruel lie is told them, that we deprive them of labor and receive the money which would otherwise make its way into their pockets.

Sir, the Irish-American will one day find out his mistake. He will find that in assuming our avocation, he has also assumed our degradation. But for the present we are the sufferers. Our old employments by which we have been accustomed to gain a livelihood are gradually slipping from our hands. Every hour sees us elbowed out of some employment to make room for some newly-arrived emigrant from the Emerald Isle, whose hunger and color entitle him to special favor. These white men are becoming house-servants, cooks, stewards, waiters, and flunkies. For aught I see they adjust themselves to their stations with all proper humility. If they cannot rise to the dignity of white men, they show that they can fall to the degradation of black men.

But now, sir, look once more! While the colored people are thus elbowed out of employment; while a ceaseless enmity in the Irish is excited against us; while State after State enacts laws against us; while we are being hunted down like wild beasts; while we are oppressed with a sense of increasing insecurity, the American Colonization Society, with hypocrisy written on its brow, comes to the front, awakens to new life, and vigorously presses its scheme for our expatriation upon the attention of the American people. Papers have been started in the North and the South to promote this long-cherished object—to get rid of the Negro, who is presumed to be a standing menace to slavery. Each of these papers is adapted to the latitude in which it is published, but each and all are united in calling upon the government for appropriations to enable the Colonization Society to send us out of the country by steam. Evidently this society looks upon our extremity as its opportunity, and whenever the elements are stirred against us it is stimulated to unusual activity. It does not deplore our misfortunes, but rather rejoices in them, since they prove that the two races cannot flourish on the same soil.

Hinton Rowan Helper: Slavery Renounced [27]

The views of poor whites were given classical expression by Hinton Rowan Helper (1829–1909), a North Carolinian who sought gold in California, and brooded upon the existence of slavery as having foisted an inferior race upon the southern states to their moral and economic detriment and the oppression of his own class of free white labor. He published in 1857 The Impending Crisis: How to Meet It. *Helper's hatred of slaveholders, whom he accused of having deceived his people respecting the productivity of land worked by slaves, made him an exile from the South and an abolitionist able to affect northern opinion which was concerned with freedom, rather than with the well-being of Negroes.* The Impending Crisis, *circulating in the millions of copies throughout the northern states, became a powerful tool of Republicans during the Presidential election of 1860. In the South, the book was proscribed.*

We are credibly informed that many of the farmers in the immediate vicinity of Baltimore, where we now write, have turned their attention exclusively to hay, and that from one acre they frequently gather two tons, for which they receive *fifty dollars.* Let us now inquire how many dollars may be expected from an acre planted in cotton. Mr. Cameron, from whose able address before the Agricultural Society of Orange County, North Carolina, we have already gleaned some interesting particulars, informs us, that the cotton planters in his part of the country, "have contented themselves with a crop yielding only *ten or twelve dollars per acre,*" and that "the summing up of a large surface gives but a living result." An intelligent resident of the Palmetto State, writing in De Bow's Review, not long since, advances the opinion that the cotton

[27] Hinton Rowan Helper, *Compendium of the Impending Crisis of the South* (New York, 1860), 30–31, 60–61.

planters of South Carolina are not realizing more than *one per cent.* on the amount of capital they have invested. While in Virginia, very recently, an elderly slaveholder, whose religious walk and conversation had recommended and promoted him to an eldership in the Presbyterian church, and who supports himself and family by raising negroes and tobacco, told us that, for the last eight or ten years, aside from the increase of his human chattels, he felt quite confident *he had not cleared as much even as one per cent. per annum* on the amount of his investment. The real and personal property of this aged *Christian* consists chiefly in a large tract of land and about thirty negroes, most of whom, according to his own confession, are more expensive than profitable. The proceeds arising from the sale of the tobacco they produce, are all absorbed in the purchase of meat and bread for home consumption, and when the crop is stunted by drought, frost, or otherwise cut short, one of the negroes must be sold to raise funds for the support of the others. Such are the agricultural achievements of slave labor; such are the results of "the sum of all villainies." The diabolical institution subsists on its own flesh. At one time children are sold to procure food for the parents, at another, parents are sold to procure food for the children. Within its pestilential atmosphere, nothing succeeds; progress and prosperity are unknown; inanition and slothfulness ensue; everything becomes dull, dismal and unprofitable; wretchedness and desolation stand or lie in bold relief throughout the land; an aspect of most melancholy inactivity and dilapidation broods over every city and town; ignorance and prejudice sit enthroned over the minds of the people; usurping despots wield the sceptre of power; everywhere, and in everything, between Delaware Bay and the Gulf of Mexico, are the multitudinous evils of slavery apparent. . . .

Non-slaveholders of the South! farmers, mechanics and workingmen, we take this occasion to assure you that the slaveholding politicians whom you have elected to offices of honor and profit, have hoodwinked you, trifled with you, and used you as mere tools for the consummation of their wicked designs. They have purposely kept you in ignorance, and have, by molding your passions and prejudices to suit themselves, induced you to act in direct opposition to your dearest rights and interests. By a system of the grossest subterfuge and misrepresentation, and in order to avert, for a season, the vengeance that will most assuredly overtake them ere long, they have taught you to hate the lovers of liberty, who are your best and only true friends. Now, as one of your own number, we appeal to you to join us in our earnest and timely efforts to rescue the generous soil of the South from the usurped and desolating control of these political vampires. Once and forever, at least so far as this country is concerned, the infernal question of slavery must be disposed of; a speedy and absolute abolishment of the whole system is the true policy of the South—and this is the policy which we propose to pursue. Will you aid us, will you assist us, will you be freemen, or will you be slaves? These are questions of vital importance; weigh them well in your minds; come to a prudent and firm decision, and hold yourselves in readiness to act in accordance therewith. You must either be for us or against us—anti-slavery or pro-slavery; it is impossible for you to occupy a neutral ground; it is as certain as fate itself, that if you do not voluntarily oppose the usurpations and outrages of the slavocrats, they will force you into involuntary compliance with their infamous measures. Consider well the aggressive, fraudulent and despotic power which they have exercised in the affairs of Kansas; and remember that, if, by adhering to erroneous principles of neutrality or non-resistance, you allow them to force the curse of slavery on that or any other vast and fertile field, the broad area of all the surrounding States and Territories—the whole nation, in fact—will soon fall a prey to their diabolical intrigues and machinations. Thus, if you are not vigilant, will they take advantage of your neutrality, and make you and others the victims of their inhuman despotism. Do not reserve the strength of your arms until you shall have been rendered powerless to strike; the present is the proper time for action; under all the circumstances, apathy or indifference is a crime. First ascertain, as nearly as you can, the precise nature and extent of your duty, and then, without a moment's delay, perform it in good faith. To facilitate you in determining what considerations of right, justice and humanity require at your hands, is one of the primary objects of this work; and we shall certainly fail in our desire if we do not accomplish our task in a manner acceptable to God and advantageous to man.

Emancipation: The Confederate Program[28]

To be fully appreciated, Lincoln's tactics and strategy need to be compared with those which the Confederate leadership proposed, and would have furthered, had their armies attained their goals.

The public journals of the North have been received, containing a proclamation dated on the first day of the present month, signed by the President of the United States, in which he orders and declares all slaves within ten of the States of the Confederacy to be free, except such as are found within certain districts now occupied in part by the armed forces of the enemy.

We may well leave it to the instincts of that common humanity which a beneficent Creator has implanted in the breasts of our fellow-men of all countries to pass judgment on a measure by which several millions of human beings of an inferior race, peaceful and contented laborers in their sphere, are doomed to extermination, while at the same time they are encouraged to a general assassination of their masters by the insidious recommendation "to abstain from violence unless in necessary self-defense." Our own detestation of those who have attempted the most execrable measure recorded in the history of guilty man is tempered by profound contempt for the impotent rage which it discloses. So far as regards the action of this Government on such criminals as may attempt its execution, I confine myself to informing you that I shall, unless in your wisdom you deem some other course more expedient, deliver to the several State authorities all commissioned officers of the United States that may hereafter be captured by our forces in any of the States embraced in the proclamation, that they may be dealt with in accordance

[28] *Journal of the Congress of the Confederate States of America 1861–1865* (Washington, D.C., 1904), III, 17–18.

with the laws of those States providing for the punishment of criminals engaged in exciting servile insurrection. The enlisted soldiers I shall continue to treat as unwilling instruments in the commission of these crimes, and shall direct their discharge and return to their homes on the proper and usual parole.

In its political aspect this measure possesses great significance, and to it in this light I invite your attention. It affords to our whole people the complete and crowning proof of the true nature of the designs of the party which elevated to power the present occupant of the Presidential chair at Washington, and which sought to conceal its purposes by every variety of artful device and by the perfidious use of the most solemn and repeated pledges on every possible occasion. I extract, in this connection, as a single example, the following declaration made by President Lincoln, under the solemnity of his oath as Chief Magistrate of the United States, on the 4th March, 1861:

"Apprehension seems to exist among the people of the Southern States that by the accession of a Republican Administration their property and their peace and personal security are to be endangered. There has never been any reasonable cause for such apprehensions. Indeed, the most ample evidence to the contrary has all the while existed and been open to their inspection. It is found in nearly all the published speeches of him who now addresses you. I do but quote from one of those speeches when I declare that I have no purpose, directly or indirectly, to interfere with the institution of slavery in the States where it exists. I believe I have no lawful right to do so, and I have no inclination to do so. Those who nominated and elected me did so with full knowledge that I had made this and many similar declarations, and had never recanted them. And, more than this, they placed in the platform for my acceptance, and as a law to themselves and to me, the clear and emphatic resolution which I now read:

" 'Resolved, That the maintenance inviolate of the rights of the States, and especially the right of each State to order and control its own domestic institutions according to its own judgment exclusively, is essential to the balance of powers on which the perfection and endurance of our political fabric depend; and we denounce the lawless invasion by armed force of the soil of any State or Territory, no matter under what pretext, as among the gravest crimes.' "

Nor was this declaration of the want of power or disposition to interfere with our social system confined to a state of peace. Both before and after the actual commencement of hostilities the President of the United States repeated in formal official communication to the cabinets of Great Britain and France that he was utterly without constitutional power to do the act which he has just committed, and that in no possible event, whether the secession of these States resulted in the establishment of a separate confederacy or in the restoration of the Union, was there any authority by virtue of which he could either restore a disaffected State to the Union by force of arms or make any change in any of its institutions. I refer especially for verification of this assertion to the dispatches addressed by the Secretary of State of the United States, under direction of the President, to the ministers of the United States at London and Paris, under date of 10th and 22d April, 1861.

The people of this Confederacy, then, can not fail to receive this proclamation as the fullest vindication of their own sagacity in foreseeing the uses to which the dominant party in the United States intended from the beginning to apply their power, nor can they cease to remember, with devout thankfulness, that it is to their own vigilance in resisting the first stealthy progress of approaching despotism that they owe their escape from consequences now apparent to the most skeptical. This proclamation will have another salutary effect in calming the fears of those who have constantly evinced the apprehension that this war might end by some reconstruction of the old Union or some renewal of close political relations with the United States. These fears have never been shared by me, nor have I ever been able to perceive on what basis they could rest. But the proclamation affords the fullest guarantee of the impossibility of such a result; it has established a state of things which can lead to but one of three possible consequences—the extermination of the slaves, the exile of the whole white population from the Confederacy, or absolute and total separation of these States from the United States.

This proclamation is also an authentic statement by the Government of the United States of its inability to subjugate the South by force of arms, and as such must be accepted by neutral nations, which can no longer find any justification in withholding our just claims to formal recognition. It is also in effect an intimation to the people of the North that they must prepare to submit to a separation, now become inevitable, for that people are too acute not to understand that a restoration of the Union has been rendered forever impossible by the adoption of a measure which, from its very nature, neither admits of retraction nor can coexist with union.

Slavery in Retrospect: The Freedman[29]

*Post-slavery writings and reminiscences regarding the institution served
many purposes, from the complex and artistic "Uncle Remus" tales of Joel
Chandler Harris to the self-serving apologetics of the Virginia novelist
Thomas Nelson Page. Some of the keenest reminiscences came from the ex-
slaves themselves, and ranged from accounts of personal vicissitudes to com-
mentary on the social system of which they had once been part. They ranged,
too, from fond recollections of slavery days to bitter memories and scorn of
oppressors. Not infrequently, positive and negative memories mingled, and
were succeeded by a concern for new problems and interests, as in the case of
a Kentucky slave who became a Federal soldier and later settled in Tennessee.*

It was a long, long time before everything got quiet after the War. On
Franklin Street here I saw once 100 Ku Klux Klans, with long robes and
faces covered. You don't know anything of them. They were going down
here a piece to hang a man. There were about 600 of us soldiers, so we
followed them to protect the man. The Klan knew this and passed on by
the house and went on back to town and never did bother the man.

One time a colored soldier married a white woman over here at Fort
Bruce. The man belonged to my company. His name was Sergeant
Cook. About twenty of the soldiers went to the wedding, and they had
about five or six white men who said he couldn't marry this woman. Old
Dr. Taylor (and by the way this Tāylor's Hill here is named for him)
came over to marry them. He stood near me and I told him to go on and
marry this couple or else someone here would die. He looked around

---

[29] "Unwritten History of Slavery; Autobiographical Account of Negro
Ex-Slaves. Social Science Source Documents No. 1" (Fisk University,
Nashville, Tenn., 1945), mimeo., 123–124, 126–127.

and saw all these soldiers and he knew about us and that we meant for
him to do as he had been told. He married them and we guarded their
hack over to the war boat on the cumberland. They went over to Nashville and lived there. They had a daughter whose name was Mrs. Gnatt.
When they married was in 1866. Mrs. Gnatt could tell you her father
was named Cyrus Cook. Guess you know you can't do that now, no sir;
you just can't do that now. At one time a colored man could ride anywhere he wanted to, but now he can't do it. I am one of the first voters of
Montgomery County. They told me at one time that I was not to come
to the polls or I would be met by 600 men on horses. So about six or
eight hundred of us armed and went to the polls with our bayonets. That
man that had told me that did not show up. So we voted, and voted for
whom we wanted. . . .

When I first came here we had no teachers here but white teachers.
They would call the roll same as calling the roll for soldiers. They taught
school in the churches before they had school houses. They used to go to
school at night and work all day. Clarence C. White's father, Will White,
was the first teacher or principal of the school here in Clarksville. Ed
White, his brother, was shot and killed in Topeka, Kansas, and brought
here to be buried. He has a daughter in Fisk University now who is a
matron or something, I don't know exactly.

In those times some people married just like we marry now, only they
didn't get a license but they would get permission from their owner first
and then from the girl's parents. Sometimes they got a preacher to marry
them, and sometimes they jumped over the broom stick. When they were
married by a preacher, they called that a lawful marriage, and when the
War come up if a soldier died the wife could get a pension; but if they
married by jumping over the broom stick, they didn't recognize that if a
soldier died, and his wife could get nothing. . . .

As it is now, I sit down and talk to these old Rebel white people about
how they used to do. I treat everybody right; I hold nothing against
them. I used to drive a hack here, and would get about as many white
passengers as the white hack drivers got. One time a white man came
over to my hack and asked me whose hack it was, and I told him that it
was Mr. Farley's, and he said, "Well, how much for a trip?" and I told
him 50 cents. After I made the trip he said, "Here is 50 cents for your
boss and $1.00 for you." He was supposed to be a wealthy man, and I
was glad to get that $1.50. Mr. Farley was myself, but he didn't know it,
so I didn't tell him nothing but the truth and got $1.50.

One time a white man came to my house and said he was coming to
whip me. So when he came I saw a man come loping up on a horse, and
I got two pistols, one in my right hand and one in my pocket, and went
out to the gate, and he asked me what was the matter with me. I grabbed

the horse and threw the pistol in his face and told him I would show him. So he said, "That's all right, that's all right," and when I turned his horse aloose, he galloped off. . . .

When the War was over some of the colored returned to their white folks, but I didn't want to be under the white folks again. I was glad to get out. Once, for fifteen years here, I run a saloon and livery stable. One time I worked on a boat. When I was on my first boat, one time I went to vote. A white man told me that if I voted Republican he would fire me, so I told him to fire me then. I just told him he could fire me right now for I didn't want to work anyway. I went on and voted the Republican ticket, and they told me they liked my principle and I could go on and go to work.

Slavery in Retrospect:
Henry A. Wise Assayed [30]

A curiosity of post-Civil War semantics is the fact that "scalawag"—a term scornfully applied by southern whites to other southern whites who co-operated with Federal Reconstructionists—became a contemptuous term in the North as well. Although Confederates had claimed to be part of a new nation, many of them had maintained a reverence for the American Revolution and the Constitution, and they readily resumed life under the reconstructed government, asking only for the privilege of reinvigorating their battle for states rights. A key figure of the embattled South had been Henry A. Wise (1806–1876), a Virginian of eloquence who had once aspired to the Presidency. As governor of Virginia he interposed himself fatefully in the case of John Brown, refusing the support of northerners anxious to help prove that Brown had acted insanely at Harpers Ferry and ought not to be considered as typical of northern opinion. Wise saw to it that Brown was hanged, rather than incarcerated, and thus helped bring on the war. In assessing Wise's career, his grandson Barton H. Wise, also judged the work of others of Wise's generation.

Probably no man realized more keenly than Wise the ill effects of slavery, and how it had retarded the development of his State and section. He had, along with many men of his time, favored the African [American] Colonization Society, and while in Brazil had labored for the repression of the slave-trade there. In the Virginia Convention of 1850–51, he had told some plain, blunt truths in regard to the workings of the institution; and a man who declared that "black slaves make white

[30] Barton H. Wise, *The Life of Henry A. Wise* (New York, 1899), 409–413.

slaves" could hardly believe in the institution *per se*. Yet it must be said that it is by no means difficult to quote numerous extracts from his speeches and writings, from the tone of which it would appear equally, if not more, natural to arrive at exactly the opposite conclusion; and he engaged at times in much wild and extravagant talk. His excitable temper and disposition, when irritated, to run into extremes are largely the explanation of this, and are the only sort of excuse, too, that can be given for his having indulged, just prior to the war, in some of the silly attempts made among a certain class of Southern people to disparage Yankee courage. Wise was essentially a type, although an extreme one, of the defiant attitude of the South of 1860, and bitterly resented outside interference with that which he considered peculiarly a State and not a national question, and from interfering with which it was the duty of the North to abstain. In common with the best men of his generation in the South he loved the Union of the States, and impartial history will record of the Southern man of 1861 that it was the growth of circumstances beyond his power to control which placed him in conflict with that government to the support of which he had contributed even more than his share of patriotism. "As to patriotism in the broadest sense, that is, belief in American institutions, there is no better patriot in the land than the Southern man, and, paradoxical as it sounds, he was never more intensely American than when he was trying to divide the United States that he might have a place where he could work out his own interpretation of these ideas without interference." * It has been said of the antebellum Southern leader that he never rose to the national conception of the Constitution, and that his talents were those which tend to conserve existing institutions merely. It would not be difficult to point out many fallacies in these statements; but if he failed to perceive what some writers term the *growth* of the Constitution, and still adhered to the old landmarks, a disposition to "prove all things" may be as much of a virtue as an error, in a government which has been described as carrying more sail than anchor. If in the eyes of his opponents he laid too much stress upon the letter of the law and seemed at times to forget that the Constitution, like the Sabbath, was made for man, he was but following the teaching of his Revolutionary sires when, finding his rights disregarded, he fell back upon that fundamental organic law which he had been taught to reverence as the sheet anchor of our safety. . . .

In a speech delivered at Roanoke College, Salem, Virginia, on June 17, 1873, Wise gave utterance to the following views in regard to the war between the States: "The time has not yet come to view that war calmly

---

* "The Old South Still," by Captain Edward Field, Fourth Artillery U.S. Army, *United Service Magazine* February, 1896.

and philosophically. But this I will venture to say of it now: that it did what no other human power could have done,—it cauterized and cured the worst curse upon some of the fairest portions of the continent, and removed the only incubus upon the development of the southern part of the Eastern Terminus of the Great Belt. One of nature's poems is *flowing water,* with power in its current to clarify itself and purify its springs and streams. The stagnant pool is thick, malarious, and fetid; but springs and streams are usually clear and clean, and life-giving and life-sustaining. So with the watershed of this continent; it cleared and cleansed its Southern Geography of the malaria of African bondage. That cause alone made the Southern States stagnant. The globe would not be habitable, if its oceans were not agitated by storms, evaporated by the sun, congealed by frost, and cleansed by perpetual currents. And as of the currents of air and of the waters, it may be said, that they often conflict with each other, yet their very cyclones and whirlpools are made by God's providence to give motion and purification and life; so of our Civil War it may be said, I hope, in time to come, that it gave a New Life to the country and all its parts, which may atone for the many precious lives which were taken away by its fire and sword. Nothing but intraterritorial war could have given this New Life; and it was sent by God, not only because the Exodus of Slavery had come, but to make the motion of commerce and arts and migration southward. The two Virginias will now be filled with population from abroad and from other States at home, and the whole South will soon be strong enough to do a great moral duty on their part." As his purpose had never been originally to secede from the Union, so he believed that the destiny of his people was wrapped up in its future, and were he alive he could with truth repeat the lines of his friend, James Barron Hope:—

> "Give us back the ties of Yorktown,
> Perish all the modern hates;
>
> The safety of the Union
> Is the safety of the States!"

He had an abiding faith in the principles for which the South had fought as he conceived them, and never doubted that they would in the end triumph, if constitutional liberty is perpetuated in America.

The Continuing Problem of Slavery:

The Case of Liberia[31]

Although the League of Nations became notorious as a do-nothing organization, its defenders argued that no intermediary agency could be stronger than its components. The League's Temporary Slavery Commission, set up in 1924, accomplished little besides defining forms of slavery and means of enslavement, indicating areas of the world subject to the slave traffic and institutions, and soliciting the adherence of nations to its abolitionist goals. The case of Liberia, though it involved a small nation, was peculiarly relevant to the United States, which had sponsored its birth and maintained social and economic relations with it.

F. The Commission of Enquiry in Liberia

47. Amongst those documents presented by the Council to the Assembly in its annual report on 11 June 1931, was the report of the International Commission of Enquiry in Liberia (C.658.M.272.1930.VI; 1930.VI.B.6). This was a special international commission which had been set up under the authority of the Government of Liberia, with the co-operation and participation of the League of Nations, to inquire into certain allegations which had been made as to conditions of slavery and forced labour alleged to be present in that country. It was not a direct Commission of the League, but its report was submitted to the League by the Liberian Government for information and discussion.

48. By letter dated 16 September 1929 to the President of the Council

---

[31] *The Suppression of Slavery* (*Memorandum Submitted by the Secretary-General*) *United Nations—Economic and Social Council* (New York, 1951), 38–39.

of the League (A.81.1929.VI.; C.446.1929.VI), the Government of Liberia reported that it had decided to lay before the International Commission of Enquiry the question of slavery and forced labour in Liberia and accordingly set up a Commission of three members, one appointed by the Council of the League, one by the United States of America, and an ex-President of Liberia appointed by the Government of Liberia.

49. The Commission functioned from April 1930 and submitted its report to the Liberian Government on 8 September 1930. Its report which was transmitted to the Secretary-General of the League by the Liberian Government on 15 December 1930 held that certain charges against some officials of the Liberian Government were substantiated, and that in some cases there had been in Liberia forced labour differing little from conditions of slavery (C.658.M.272.1930.VI).

50. A number of important officials in Liberia including the President and Vice-President of the Republic resigned from their posts. The new Government accepted in principle the recommendations of the Commission, and passed a number of new laws in pursuance of those recommendations, in particular, Acts prohibiting the export of contract labour overseas, providing for the administrative reorganization of the hinterland, and forbidding pawning of persons, and requested the assistance of the League in the carrying out of the proposed reforms (letter of 9 January 1931, 1931.VI.B.1).

51. The Council thereupon set up a special Committee of eight of its own members to examine the request for assistance, and the conditions giving rise to the request (resolution of 24 January 1931, *Official Journal 1931*, page 219). This Committee was of opinion that the help of technical experts was necessary in order to draw up a concrete plan of assistance to be given to the Liberian Government, and obtained the appointment of a Commission of three experts, having special qualifications in general administration, financial, and health matters respectively (*Official Journal 1931*, pages 1448–1449).

52. This Commission, after both preliminary documentary study and study in Liberia itself, presented a draft plan to the Committee of the Council laying down guiding principles for the administration of the provinces, as well as concrete proposals, including recommendations concerning the principles to be applied in the application of laws concerning slavery and forced labour (*Official Journal 1932*, page 1413).

53. Three years of negotiation took place between the Committee of the Council and the Government of Liberia in the hope of reaching an agreement on the details of the plan for financial assistance to Liberia (*Official Journal 1933*, Draft Protocol establishing plan). In May 1934, however, no agreement had been arrived at, and the Council resolved to withdraw its offer of assistance, and the work of the special Committee of the Council ended.

54. Since the report of the International Commission of Enquiry in Liberia had been referred to a Special Committee of the Council set up to examine conditions in Liberia, slavery questions in that country were not dealt with by any general committee on slavery during the functioning of that Committee (A.34.1932.VI).

The Continuing Problem of Slavery:
The United Nations[32]

*The United Nations General Assembly in 1948 accepted a Universal Dec-
laration of Human Rights, drafted by a U.N. Commission on Human Rights
headed by Eleanor Roosevelt. It included the statement (Art. 4) that "[n]o
one shall be held in slavery or servitude; slavery and the slave trade shall be
prohibited in all their forms." Nevertheless, there having been no enforcement machinery provided, it added still another statement of moral intent to
the many which preceded it. Actual implementation of the Declaration proceeded at a slow pace, as indicated by one of the United Nations reports.*

UNITED NATIONS CONFERENCE
ON PLENIPOTENTIARIES

The United Nations Conference of Plenipotentiaries on a Supplementary Convention on the Abolition of Slavery, the Slave Trade and Institutions and Practices Similar to Slavery met at the European Office of
the United Nations in Geneva from 13 August to 4 September 1956.
Fifty-one States sent representatives to participate in the Conference,
and eight sent observers.

The Conference adopted, by a vote of 40 to 0, with 3 abstentions, a
Supplementary Convention on the Abolition of Slavery, the Slave Trade
and Institutions and Practices Similar to Slavery. It also adopted two
recommendations. One was that States who would become parties to the
Supplementary Convention should, if they have not already done so, accede to the Slavery Convention of 1926, as amended by the Protocol of
1953. The other recommendation was that the Economic and Social

[32] *Yearbook of the United Nations 1956* (New York, 1957), 228–229.

Council consider the appropriateness of initiating a study on the question of marriage with the object of drawing attention to the desirability of having the free consent of both parties to a marriage and of the establishment of a minimum age for marriage, preferably not less than 14 years.

The Supplementary Convention lays down that States Parties should take measures to bring about progressively and as soon as possible the complete abolition or abandonment of certain institutions and practices, such as debt bondage, serfdom, bride-price and exploitation of child labour (article 1). It favours the prescription of suitable minimum ages of marriage and the registration of marriages; emphasizes the criminality of the slave trade; and provides sanctions for other related practices. It also provides for the co-operation of States Parties with each other and with the United Nations, and for communication to the Secretary-General of the United Nations of information on laws, regulations and administrative measures enacted to implement the Convention. No reservations are permitted. Disputes relating to interpretation or application of the Convention may be referred by any of the parties to the dispute to the International Court of Justice, unless another mode of settlement is agreed upon. The Convention is to apply *ipso facto* to all Non-Self-Governing, Trust, colonial and other non-metropolitan Territories of a State Party, except in cases where the previous consent of the non-metropolitan Territory is required by the constitutional laws and practices of the Party or of the Territory concerned.

The Convention was signed on 7 September, 1956, by the following 33 States: Australia, Belgium, Byelorussian SSR, Canada, Czechoslovakia, El Salvador, France, Federal Republic of Germany, Greece, Guatemala, Haiti, Hungary, India, Iraq, Israel, Italy, Liberia, Luxembourg, Mexico, Netherlands, Norway, Pakistan, Peru, Poland, Portugal, Romania, San Marino, Sweden, Ukrainian SSR, USSR, United Kingdom, Viet-Nam and Yugoslavia. The Convention will remain open for signature until 1 July 1957, by any Member of the United Nations or specialized agency. Thereafter it will be open for accession by any Member of the United Nations or specialized agency or by any other State invited by the United Nations General Assembly to accede. It will enter into force as soon as two States have become parties thereto.

Recommended Reading

Abel, A. H., *The American Indian as Slaveholder and Secessionist* (Cleveland, 1915).

Andrews, E. A., *Slavery and the Domestic Slave-Trade in the United States* (Boston, 1836).

Aptheker, H., *American Negro Slave Revolts* (New York, 1943).

———, ed., *A Documentary History of the Negro People in the United States* (New York, 1951).

Bailey, L. R. *Indian Slave Trade in the Southwest* (Los Angeles, 1966).

Ballagh, J. C. *A History of Slavery in Virginia* (Baltimore, 1902).

Bancroft, F., *Slave Trading in the Old South* (Baltimore, 1931).

Bethell, L., *The Abolition of the Brazilian Slave Trade* (Cambridge, Eng., 1970).

Blake, W. O., *The History of Slavery and the Slave Trade* (Columbus, O., 1857).

Botkin, B. A., ed., *Lay My Burden Down; a Folk History of Slavery* (Chicago, 1945).

Brackett, J. R., *The Negro in Maryland* (Baltimore, 1889).

Buckingham, J. S., *The Slave States of America* (London, 1842).

Campbell, S. W., *The Slave Catchers: Enforcement of the Fugitive Slave Law, 1850–1860* (Chapel Hill, N.C., 1970).

Catterall, H. T., ed., *Judicial Cases Concerning American Slavery and the Negro* (Washington, 1929).

Cobb, T. R. R., *An Historical Sketch of Slavery* (Philadelphia, 1858).

Coleman, J. W., *Slavery Times in Kentucky* (Chapel Hill, N.C., 1940).

Conrad, A. H. and J. R. Meyer, *The Economics of Slavery, and Other Studies in Econometric History* (Chicago, 1964).

Copley, E. H., *A History of Slavery and Its Abolition* (London, 1839).

Curtin, P. D., *Two Jamaicas* (New York, 1968).

Davidson, B., *Black Mother* (Boston, 1961).

Davis, D. B., *The Problem of Slavery in Western Culture* (Ithaca, N.Y., 1966).

De Beaumont, G., *Marie, or Slavery in the United States* (Stanford, Calif., 1958).

Degler, C. N., *Neither Black nor White* (New York, 1971).

De Bow, J. D. B., *The Industrial Resources . . . Particularly of the Southern and Western States* (New York, 1966 ed.).

Díaz Soler, L. M., *Historia de la Esclavitud Negra en Puerto Rico* (Barcelona, 1970).

Dow, G. F., *Slave Ships and Slavery* (Salem, 1927).

Du Bois, W. E. B., *Suppression of the African Slave-Trade to the United States of America, 1638–1870* (New York, 1896).

Duigan, P., *The United States and the African Slave Trade, 1619–1862* (Stanford, Calif., 1963).

Elkins, S., *Slavery: A Problem in American Institutional and Intellectual Life* (Chicago, 1959).

Fernandes, F., *The Negro in Brazilian Society* (New York, 1969).

Filler, L., *Crusade Against Slavery, 1830–1860* (New York, 1971 ed.).

Fisher, A. G. B. and H. J., *Slavery and Muslim Society in Africa* (New York, 1971).

Fisher, M. M., *Negro Slave Songs in the United States* (Ithaca, N.Y., 1953).

Flanders, R. B., *Plantation Slavery in Georgia* (Chapel Hill, N.C., 1933).

Freyre, G., *The Masters and the Slaves* (New York, 1946).

Friends, Society of, *An Exposition of the African Slave Trade . . . 1840 to 1850* (Philadelphia, 1851).

Gaines, F. P., *The Southern Plantation, a Study in the Development and the Accuracy of a Tradition* (New York, 1925).

Genovese, E. D., *The Political Economy of Slavery; Studies in the Economy and Society of the Slave South* (New York, 1965).

Goodell, W., *The American Slave Code in Theory and Practice* (New York, 1853).

Goveia, E. V., *Slave Society in the British Leeward Islands* (New Haven, 1965).

Greene, L. J., *The Negro in Colonial New England, 1620–1776* (New York, 1942).

Greenridge, C. W., *Slavery* (New York, 1958).

Harris, N. D., *Slavery in Illinois* (Chicago, 1906).

Hart, A. B., *Slavery and Abolition, 1831–1841* (New York, 1906).

Herrick, C. A., *White Servitude in Pennsylvania* (Philadelphia, 1926).

Hollander, B., *Slavery in America* (New York, 1963).

Howard, Warren S., *American Slavers and the Federal Law, 1837–1862* (Berkeley, 1963).

Jenkins, W. S., *Pro-Slavery Thought in the Old South* (Chapel Hill, N.C., 1935).

Jernegan, M. W., *Laboring and Dependent Classes in Colonial America, 1607–1783* (Chicago, 1931).

Jordan, W. D., *White Over Black* (Chapel Hill, N.C., 1968).